gettingagripon PARENTING TIME

86 Commonsense Lessons from the Trenches

ROBYN PEARCE

getting agrip publishing

Published by Getting A Grip Publishing

Cover design and interior layout by Fresha Creative, www.freshacreative.co.nz
Printed by Wickliffe New Zealand, www.wickliffe.co.nz
First Published 2016
© 2016 Robyn Pearce

Photo credits: Most are from the Parsons/Pearce family archives.
p. 46-7 Karen Boyes. p. 171-2 Beth van Hulst.
p. 53 Steve Mann, 101 Szefei, used under license from Shutterstock.
Kite icon made by Freepik from www.flaticon.com

The moral rights of the author have been asserted. All rights reserved. This book or any portion thereof may not be reproduced distributed, or transmitted in any form or by any means, without the prior written permission of the publisher, except in the case of brief quotations as permitted by copyright law.
For permission requests, please contact info@gettingagrip.com.

Disclaimer

Apart from my children, close family, and contributors, most names have been changed especially those central to the various cautionary tales.
Nothing in this book is intended as a substitute for the advice of qualified clinicians of physical or mental sciences. The reader should regularly consult a physician in matters relating to their family's health and particularly with respect to any symptoms that may require diagnosis or medical attention

Every effort has been made to contact copyright holders of any quoted text.

Resources

Get your free report *'How To Master Time In Only 90 Seconds'* and regular useful time tips and inspiration at www.gettingagrip.com

ISBN: 978-0-9582460-2-6 (Paperback edition)
ISBN: 978-0-9582460-6-4 (eBook edition)

Find this book at www.gettingagrip.com/products/books or a reputable bookshop near you.

For bulk and wholesale orders contact office@gettingagrip.com

Also available on Amazon.

Gifts for you

We have an extra bonus for you - some pearls of wisdom learnt from five of the world's top thought leaders on efficiency and productivity.

Grab their wisdom *now* with this free audio download http://gettingagrip.com/digitalgifts on how to make time for exercise; how to control your inbox; and practical advice on goals, simplicity, managing major projects and more.

To my wonderful children – you have all taught me so much.

*My daughter Catherine Heineke, my sons
Chris, Graham, James and Maurice Parsons, and my foster son
Paul Stidder, who lived with us for all his school years.*

*And to the beloved 17, in age order:
Sam, Reuben, Hannah, Callum, Joel, Corin, Luke, Ethan, Matt,
Alisha, Lachlan, Brianna, Sophia, Joseph, Olivia, Liam and Bethany.*

*You are our future.
Good luck with teaching your parents.*

My inspiration

WHAT READERS SAY

This book is Robyn's finest work to date. With her tribe of children and 17 grandchildren as evidence, Robyn has cleverly combined her professional acumen with her experience of life to produce this wonderfully practical parenting handbook. **Yvonne Godfrey**, *Founder of MIOMO (Making It On My Own), host parent on reality TV show, The World's Strictest Parents, author of Parenting Yadults – How to Set Up Your Young Adult for Independence and Success in Life!*

Another great informative read from the Time Queen. Robyn has woven her personal parenting experiences and observations with lessons learned from others to produce a book of great tips, advice and learning. This book will challenge your assumptions and parenting style to strengthen your bond between you and your child. I will be personally using some of the superb tips to become a better parent to my two children. **Karen Tui Boyes**, *Spectrum Education. Educator, Speaker & Author.*

This book has common sense, practical advice that all parents can relate to, with lots of easy tips which can be incorporated into our daily routine. I look forward to sharing the ideas. **Linda Venables**, *Regional Manager, Radius Residential Care, New Zealand.*

Robyn's many years as a mother and grandmother means she writes from her personal experiences, rather than basing her work on the second-hand telling of episodes and events of others. Her book should be essential reading for all parents, no matter their age. **Phillipa Challis**, *Live Life Laughing, Australia.*

What a heap of wonderful and VERY practical observations, suggestions and useful advice, supported by research, to guide even the most confused parent and every family, regardless of age and stage of children, (even for grannies!). All presented in a very readable style – exactly what you would expect from Robyn. I loved the concept of computer dollars. What an easy way to reinforce the idea that family life is made up of responsibilities as well as privileges. And sick of your children whinging because they're not getting what they want? Check out Lesson 19 on lessons learnt from the French. What a pity Robyn wasn't writing when I was bringing up my children - I would have had a lot more answers! **Anna Ryan**, *Ryan Publications.*

Thank you, thank you, thank you for all your wonderful, thoughtful, insightful tips. I think the biggest benefits from reading your book is knowing that I'm not alone in this crazy juggle, and that someone has taken the time to test, measure & report quicker and more time effective ways of getting all those routine but vitally important jobs done. You've shaved minutes of work from each of my days, and I'm so proud I'm finally getting a handle on it all. **Helen Faulkner**, *The Saddle Camp, Australia.*

Robyn has provided practical tips and suggestions for saving time and managing children. Her experience with her own tribe clearly shows through and she has found tips and suggestions from a wide range of other sources. Even if you don't agree with all of Robyn's advice, each point she makes invites discussion and deep thought for the reader and their parenting community. A good read to dip in and out of, and excellent references for other reading. Highly recommended. **Lisa Rose**, *mother of six and blogger.*

As a self-employed, single parent of many years, I am often purely in "survival mode." It is very easy to feel riddled with guilt and second guess yourself around how you are raising your children. This is an enjoyable and refreshing read. A mix of story-telling, statistical evidence, and no-nonsense practical help, all sprinkled with her motherly and grandmotherly love. Robyn gets it! Reading this book has allowed me to acknowledge I'm not doing so badly after all and has given me some *more great tools – no guilt attached.* **Simonne Liley**, *Practice Manager.*

I am half way through your book and I love it! I have laughed so many times already. This is really such a cool book, with heaps of humour. **Charlene Lucas.**

I like that the common sense approach, referenced to research findings, is backed by her personal stories/experiences and thoughtful reasoning. An example is the excerpt about boys' need for risk and challenges. **Christine Scothern.**

Good pace, easy reading style, great information/research/stories and great ideas for involving children and 'grandies'. **Ros Colquhoun.**

– CONTENTS –

A PEEK INTO THIS BOOK 9

SECTION I:
Start as you mean to go on - reflections on effective parenting 15

SECTION II
Top-level habits for better family-time effectiveness 68

SECTION III
Time out for frazzled and exhausted parents 91

SECTION IV
Tips and techniques for daily efficiencies: 112

SECTION V:
Fast and healthy food - yes, you can have both at the same time! 148

– BONUS SECTIONS –

SECTION VI:
A few observations on technology overuse 173

SECTION VII:
Raising teenagers without pulling your hair out 184

SECTION VIII:
Time management tips for everyone, not just parents and caregivers 213

LOVE IS EVERYTHING 244

ACKNOWLEDGEMENTS, BIBLIOGRAPHY AND USEFUL RESOURCES 246

A PEEK INTO THIS BOOK

Greetings to you all - mums, dads, grandparents, aunties and uncles, caregivers and anyone else with an interest in seeing our children grow up to be responsible members of society.

This book started many years ago as articles in a range of magazines, my weekly column in the online version of the New Zealand Herald and my blog (which you'll find at www.gettingagrip.com). Think of it as a collection of lessons learnt on the job – the hard way!

After much nagging from friends around the world, I've been persuaded to strap these 'babies' into a digital car-seat, give them a polish up, add more content and send them out in grown-up form – a book – into our wonderful wired world. (Words, sit still while I belt you in!)

Have fun with it. You might not agree with all my philosophies and ideas; I don't promise to be politically correct. They've worked for me but that's not to say they'll work for every parent, caregiver or child. I haven't tried to cover every aspect of child-raising – that would require an encyclopaedia! Instead, you'll discover my home-grown philosophies, organically gathered over many years, from my perspective as a time management specialist, parent and grandmother.

There's never enough time!

Have you noticed a common theme in society today? There never seems to be enough time in the day for everything, or so we believe. (I don't buy into that philosophy, as you'll read further on.)

If you're a parent or regular caregiver you probably collapse into bed at night dreaming wistfully of the day when you'll have some time to yourself. You love your children, you can't imagine life without them, but oh for the chance to have an uninterrupted meal. You wonder when you'll next enjoy a bath without someone thumping on the door. You wish you could go to the toilet without *'Hurry up Mum, I'm busting'* shouted through the door with rising anxiety or *'Dad, Johnny hit me'* bellowed from the other end of the house. And the thought of having a quiet sit-down seems like a distant memory; 'quiet' and 'children' don't often belong in the same sentence!

Hang in there. Our babies grow up very fast. One day the noise and mess will disappear. Enjoy the chaotic and crazy years. This is your opportunity to make a difference as you guide and grow young people into valuable, well-adjusted members of society.

What gives me the right to talk about raising kids?

I've birthed five and raised six. (Paul is an intellectually handicapped foster son who came to us at the age of three and is now living happily in a semi-independent living environment.)

Somewhere we missed on the gender balance. Five of the six are boys and now they're continuing the family trend. These days I'm blessed with a very large number of grandchildren – I think we *might* be at the end with 17! Eleven of them are that same dirty, noisy, rambunctious species – delicious boys. I'm also regularly involved with two lovely great-nieces who have no grandparents living anywhere nearby.

You'll find here the thoughts, philosophies and time-saving strategies of a practical country woman who grew up with no luxuries. After 15 years of marriage to a farmer I found myself a single mum on government welfare for the next four years, 'job-sharing' the raising of the children with their father, who has been a very dedicated dad.

The first part-time job I had while on welfare was house-cleaning to scrape together a few extra dollars for necessities.

Many times I wondered how I was going to pay the bills. But now, looking back, I'm glad for the journey. Of my five birth children, two are army officers (the oldest is currently a brigadier and the youngest is a major), another son is a country policeman and the fourth is a sheep-and-beef farmer and a leader in New Zealand agri-politics. Their sister and my only daughter works with her husband, running the administration side of their family building business.

Our tough and penny-pinching life when they were young has given them great skills in resilience, adaptability and a strong work ethic. I'm very proud of my kids and have a wonderful relationship with all of them. It is also a delight to see the way they relate to their children; they're great parents. Being the offspring of divorced parents has certainly not consigned them to a dysfunctional adulthood.

There is life after babies and the chaos of small children!

If you're a young parent right now, does it ever feel like you'll spend the rest of your natural days in crazy mode? I know I felt that way – for years. People said there was a light at the end of the tunnel but all I saw was a fog – of exhaustion and endless chores. While it was accented by lots of fun, laughs and love for my children, it was a fog nonetheless.

To be sure, I still have the occasional stint of changing nappies, wiping noses, feeding the troops and keeping the peace, but only when a parcel of small darlings is left with me while their exhausted parents take a few days' holiday. And there is a return address on the parcel!

Here's a thumbnail sketch of my 'post-childraising' life as encouragement for you.

Life is very different from those broke and penniless days surviving on government assistance in the Far North of New Zealand. Since the early 1990s I've been a writer, speaker, media presenter, trainer and consultant/coach on all aspects of time management, work/life balance and productivity. (You can find out about my work at www.gettingagrip.com). My biggest client group is the business world in Australia and New Zealand, with regular forays for both work and pleasure to the other side of the world – from Dubai, Africa and Asia to France and other European countries, England and the American continent.

I live in beautiful semi-rural New Zealand only 45 minutes south of Auckland, on the water's edge of a big tidal estuary. The sports I enjoy include competitive sailing with the Auckland Classic Yacht fleet, hiking, cycling, jogging and walking. The exercise is vital – it allows me to enjoy lovely wine and food without looking like a pumpkin! I'm also an avid reader.

Then there's my ongoing love affair with France. This was triggered by my fluent French-speaking daughter-in-law Lauren who did her last year of schooling as an exchange student. Her generous and delightful host parents, who live near Paris, have become part of our extended family. In his deliciously accented English, her host father Jean-Michel threw out a challenge a few years ago: *'Robyn, next time you come to France you must be speaking some French!'*

'Oui, Jean-Mi', was my response. Then I scurried around to find a French teacher in Auckland.

A few months later the local Alliance Française became a regular port of call. Now the big goal is to become fluent enough that I can communicate effectively with my growing group of French friends in their own language and in their own country.

These days I spend increasing chunks of time in France. The visits started out with a desire to build language competency. Then, in 2014 an aunt handed me one page of a sketchy family tree. I couldn't believe my eyes. We have French Huguenot ancestry! Watch this space for at least one book on that particular journey of discovery.

And, of course, I spend regular time with my adult children and rapidly growing grandkids and honorary grandkids – visiting, childminding, and having adventures together. You'll find observations and learnings from some of those interactions sprinkled through this book. Children are a great source of material!

Why did I choose time management as a career?

It chose me! If you've read any of my other books, you'll know that I didn't start off very well in the time-skills department. When I confess to this and people hear that I raised six kids, they look startled.

'Surely you must have been good at time management if you brought up that many children?' they say in shock. No, actually. I was constantly late for things, frequently lived in a muddle, and the round thing on top of my shoulders was often a confused ball of mush.

One pivotal experience in those frenetic child-raising years is etched in my memory. I'd just taken one of the ankle-biters to the toilet at a friend's house. As I pulled up his underpants, I noticed a poster on the back of the door – something about the value of time. While I can't quite recall the exact words, I do clearly remember my awareness that here was an area of life I needed to explore. I walked away telling myself I'd think about it more, when I found the time. (No, the irony has not escaped me!)

And then there was Mrs Davenport, but I'll tell you about her later.

So, we stumbled along. It wasn't until my youngest child, Maurice, was nearly 12 and I was an award-winning but burnt-out real estate agent, now living in Auckland, that a friend pointed me in the direction of a decent time management system. The knowledge was like manna from heaven. From that moment, life took a new direction – and that's another story told in other books.

You'll find a blend of two approaches scattered through this book:

1. The top-down approach: how we view time and the kind of life we want for ourselves and our families. What high level

decisions will impact the quality of our lives?

2. Practical commonsense strategies to help on a day-to-day level.

I've enjoyed this wander down memory lane as I pulled these experiences and contributions into some kind of order for you. (A bit like getting the family ready for an outing – it always takes longer than you expect!)

The Tribe

SECTION I:

START AS YOU MEAN TO GO ON – REFLECTIONS ON EFFECTIVE PARENTING

LESSON 1:

Just do your best - tomorrow is another day!

When we begin our child-raising years, doesn't it feel daunting? I'm sure I'm not the only parent to wonder if I was raising these little bundles of joy the right way. As my first son, Chris, became a curious toddler, I began to worry about all manner of things. Was I giving him enough stimulation? Was I being too strict? Was I too soft? How should I handle disobedience? How and when should I establish boundaries? What should those boundaries be? The 'should' words were many; the anxiety levels were high.

One kid turned into two, then there were three, then four and finally we stopped at five. Add a three-year-old intellectually handicapped long-term foster son before the second son was born and nine years later, to my surprise, I found six chicks in my nest. You'll appreciate why time to think about profound questions like *'Am I doing this parenting thing right?'* went down the toilet with the residue from the nappies!

When you're surrounded by a multitude of demanding little people and you're yet again pregnant and/or breastfeeding, survival becomes the key objective – no matter how many clever parenting books you've read or courses you've been to. Many days I operated on auto-pilot, parenting by default and hoping for the best. At odd moments I'd wonder how those well-organised one- or two-child families maintained such calm. And then I'd realise, *'Oh heck, two kids are painting the car* (true, that did happen), *the toddler's throwing things down the toilet and the baby needs a feed – thinking will have to wait!'*

I'm sure there were times when the people around me thought I was making mistakes with my parenting, no matter how hard I tried, but I did my weary best.

The years flashed by in a blur of small bodies, ever-empty stomachs and a permanently messy house. I got used to counting heads to make sure no-one was left behind. I got used to the bemused looks on strangers' faces as they realised this mob was all one family. And I also got used to feeling permanently out of control, always a bit behind with what needed to be done. There were never enough hours in the day and always too much to do. (Is that why I'm a time management specialist now, I wonder!)

A mother's work is never done! Embarrassing piles of washing in various stages of completion always beckoned. Curls of dust seemed to live permanently in the corners. Toys littered the floor. With eight people to clothe, the ironing and mending piles just got bigger. Outdoors, the lawns always needed mowing; the gardens seemed to be always full of weeds. And thank goodness for that long driveway – if I heard unexpected guests heading up, there was just enough time to tidy up the worst of the mess. In those two minutes I could straighten the throw-over on the shabby old sofa (all we could afford for lounge furniture)and dump unwashed dishes in the sink, pretending I was about to do them. In extreme cases I was even known to throw dirty pots and baking dishes out of sight in the oven or even the washing machine!

Of course, there was a lot of fun. Bedrooms turned into huts. Well, isn't that what blankets are for? You mean they're supposed to be on beds? Who thought of that boring idea? Pets entertained. Bonneted puppies and kittens took strolls in the dolls' pram, wheeled not just by Cathy, the one girl in the family, but also her five rowdy brothers dressed up in beads, frilly petticoats and high heels (not that they'll admit to it now!) Days after two white mice disappeared, with search parties closed down, tears wiped away and small owners resigned to their loss, they turned up (still alive, to our amazement) in a dress-up purse. Pinkie the baby possum was fun until, frightened by a dog, her strengthening and suddenly sharp claws scratched small legs as she raced for the nearest tree, which just happened to be Maurice's two-year-old head. And the hens were always underfoot. Did Graham grow up refusing to eat chicken, I wonder, because they perched on his pram at feed time? (Thank goodness Husband's bright idea to have a small free-range poultry farm didn't last more than about 18 months!)

The floor was a constant training ground for military-style obstacle courses and pitched battles of toy soldiers. (Was that what influenced two of the five boys to choose the army as a career?) Lego and Meccano pieces would turn up in the paddock, despite strict instructions that they were not be taken outside. An unsealed drive made a great mud hole for filthy small boys, aided by the hose. And of course, this mud was tracked inside unless I was very vigilant.

You get the picture, I'm sure. A fair amount of chaos was my normal daily round, but somehow I muddled through. Despite the marriage break-up, shared custody and the ongoing dramas that entailed, all the children have turned into wonderful, caring and responsible adults and are doing a great job of their own parenting. So maybe we did something right amidst all the bedlam and my concerns over discipline.

The day-to-day physical raising of children is sheer hard slog, but it's also fairly routine. Even if your house and garden sometimes look like a town tip, kids somehow get fed and clothed. Enjoy the ride, don't worry too much about the peripheral issues like housework, remember to play – and one day they'll be telling you to behave! (Yes, it has happened! A mother's revenge!)

The next generation love the dress-up box too!

LESSON 2:

Count your 'hats'

We constantly hear the work/life balance drum being beaten these days. Do you sometimes wonder if you'll ever stumble across that mystical Holy Grail of perfect life balance? Or does it seem like something that only happens for others? And if you're a parent as well as a business person does it seem like a joke?

If life is too busy, maybe it's time to step back and evaluate. Are you trying to fit too much into every day, every week?

How many roles are you currently committed to?

Take a minute to count up all the roles you juggle. The list might include parent, supporter of aging relatives, grandparent, sibling, friend, employee or employer, taxi service to various child-based activities, contributor to voluntary organisations, church or community group member, participant in sports activities … How many categories do you have? And – have you included a resting or time-out category for yourself?

We're now hearing the term *energy management* instead of just *time management*. Consider those multiple hats you wear – can you grade each on an energy ratio? Most of our close relationships are non-negotiable (sorry, you can't return that messy 12-year-old!), but what about some of the more peripheral ones?

- When do you experience your highest energy?
- What lights you up? What drains you?
- Do you find yourself reluctantly putting in the hard yards on some of those committees or activities?

- Are you feeling stretched like a sick rubber band as you run children to endless classes and events, leaving no time for relaxing?

There are no prizes for being a martyr. The kids won't suffer if they don't belong to all the same clubs and activities as Willow and Ali down the road. I've often heard young parents say, '*I want to do the best for them. If they don't get the opportunity to do* [fill in the blank] *it might spoil their chances to succeed.*'

The most important thing you can do is have a harmonious home. Stressed and exhausted parents will have grumpy, tired kids who only want you, not a million commitments. If we try to do everything we'll end up doing nothing properly. We'll also burn out, be snappy, poor company, tired parents and lovers, and less-than-effective workers.

Look for things to let go of – commitments, additional roles, projects, even magazine subscriptions – so you can have some time to relax as an individual and as a family.

See also:

Lesson 79: *Is it possible for parents to enjoy any level of work/life balance?*

LESSON 3:

Pills are not the answer

There is a serious medical trend happening throughout the Western world: the ever-growing prescription of drugs to both children and adults for depression and variations of ADHD (Attention Deficit Hyperactivity Disorder). I join many others in believing that a significant cause of this epidemic is the way many adults view time.

- Is anyone in your family impacted by depression?
- Who in your close circle takes medication in order to cope with daily living?
- What do you know about the prescribed use of amphetamines – for all ages?

If the questions above trigger a spark of interest or concern for you, please check out the Resources section at the back. I strongly recommend you investigate the books, articles and websites you'll find there.

Please be aware that I'm NOT giving medical advice. I'm not a doctor. And I recognise that for some people medication is a life-saver and a huge help.

It's over to us to moderate our children's experiences of the frenetic world we live in, but NOT with drugs.

Let's look at Ritalin, just one amphetamine that's commonly prescribed. It was first dished out to American children in 1961. Since that time there has been an epidemic of ADD diagnoses (more commonly referred to now as ADHD, although there are some differences). We probably all know children and adults who have been diagnosed with the condition and prescribed Ritalin or similar products.

How did this happen? What changed?

American psychologist Richard DeGrandpre, author of *Ritalin Nation,* believes that it's not a sudden biological mis-wiring that has caused a dramatic increase of ADHD children, but the vastly increased speed of society. There is evidence that the condition has no definite biological cause. Instead, there is growing concern that rather than the problem originating in the child's biology, rushed and stressed parents are passing on their own dysfunctional attitudes to time; are not taking the time to discipline their children properly; and are using the 'quick fix' of drugs to slow down sensory addictions caused by external influences. A two-decade study of 191 ADHD-type children showed that the way they were brought up was the issue, rather than the way their brains were wired.

From my research, it also appears that much orthodox medical training encourages practitioners to prescribe drugs to fix the symptoms they're presented with, rather than encouraging people to look at the causes. Many mental health practitioners follow the same path. Again, this is a time issue, as I'm sure you can see. Doctors are at least as time-poor as their patients.

And so the medication has become the norm. Today, many live in a world of sensory overload, of speed, and a sense of time-poverty. Technology moves faster and faster. We feel as if we can never catch up, that there is never enough time. But it's not true. Time hasn't changed – we have. We adults have choices. However, our children don't. We're the influencers who mould the behaviour of our impressionable children; the results of the wrong choices are serious.

- Many busy parents are unaware of the dangers of short-changing quality time with their children from a young age. '*I have to work to pay the bills. I'll hang out with the family when ...* [fill in the gaps].'

- Many conscientious parents think they have to give their young children every possible opportunity; what if the kid was a potential superstar in something but not enough time was invested in extending them. So parents and children hustle crazily around town, from one activity to another, with no down-time. Stress and exhaustion are a common outcome.
- Digital devices become the babysitter.
- 'Fast food' is eaten in front of square boxes spewing frenetic noise into the living rooms of the world.
- Many families don't schedule in time to talk to each other in a relaxed way. They don't even think it needs to be scheduled in, because *'we live together, don't we?'* But they're not living. They co-exist, passing like ships in the night.
- Many fathers (and not just those in big cities) only see their children on the weekends.
- Many mothers juggle jobs, kids, housework and community activities, with time for themselves a poor last.

I sincerely believe that most parents do the best they can with the resources available at the time. It may be that your family cannot survive without both parents working. Or you may be a single parent and the bread-winner of the family – I've been there.

No one book can be the magic solution for all your time problems and clearly I'm not advocating any kind of pill! Also I'm not promising you a quick fix.

Instead, I encourage you to be a seeker of solutions so that your family does not become a victim of the current epidemic of apparent time poverty. We're not time poor – that is only an illusion. We all have the same amount of time, and all the time we need to do what is really important. But – the only person who can change it for you or your children is you.

For more on causes of ADD/ADHD see also **Lesson 78:** *How good are you at multi-tasking?*

LESSON 4:

Extend those children – movement is vital

One spring I had the joy of sharing a short six kilometre overnight hike with my son Graham, his wife Tanya, and their four children on the beautiful Kepler Track in Fiordland, New Zealand.

The primary goal was to initiate their youngest son, four-year-old Liam, into hiking, one of the family's favourite outdoor activities. From Rainbow Reach carpark to Moturau Hut on the shores of Lake Manapouri is a gentle amble along well-maintained tracks carpeted with leaves from the towering canopy of beech. It's a perfect introduction for a first-time young hiker.

We had 24 wonderful hours of memory-making moments. Not only was it very special to be out in the wilderness with my family, but extended time in the beauty of Southland beech forest was a first for me.

There was also an unexpected multi-layered learning opportunity for the adults.

After leaving the hut on Sunday morning, well rested and fuelled with porridge, the children skipped off down the track. The adults were right behind. For about 20 minutes Liam kept up with his siblings, then I noticed him falling to the back of the group.

With a nod to Mum to stretch her legs and enjoy the chance to step out, I took his hand. As the rest of the family kept up their natural pace, grandmother and small boy dropped back to his preferred speed – a very leisurely suburban-style stroll.

As we ambled along, there were lengthy discussions about bush, birds and plants. Very quickly the family disappeared from sight, although for some time we could still hear them ahead. (A gang of happy kids is not a silent event, as every parent knows.)

Eventually Graham reappeared, waiting on the track for us. *'Come on, Liam, you're dawdling. You can do better than this.'*

He took his child's hand and strode off. Although Dad wanted him to learn about and enjoy the bush, he also had another more immediate agenda: to teach his child to cover distance and keep up with the rest of the family.

At first I felt a bit sorry for the child, who had to semi-jog to keep up with his long-legged father.

I wondered if Graham was being a bit tough. *'Don't you think it's a bit much to expect him to keep up with the rest of the family?'*

He replied, *'The other three were much better walkers at this age, Mum. He should be able to keep up.'*

'So why is he slower?' I asked.

'I think it's just practice. When the others were small we had to walk our dog every day and they usually came too. As soon as they could walk they did, often for an hour. But the dog was too old and frail by the time Liam came along so he hasn't done anything like as much walking. I hadn't realised how slow he would be. Maybe it's time for another dog.

'You might remember, the others were less than a year older than Liam is now when I started taking them on overnight hikes in the mountains of Tongariro National Park – and they had to carry some of their own gear. He just needs extending, then he'll find it easy to keep up.'

Liam finished the six kilometres in excellent condition, encouraged into a faster pace by both parents. He can't wait for the next adventure.

This little experience got me thinking about what we expect of our children, how easy it is to mollycoddle them, and the unintended consequences. On one level I'd just done it myself, although I certainly didn't regret it. The benefit had been a very special 45 minutes with one of my youngest grandchildren; it's a memory I'll always cherish.

Some theory behind this story

Sophie Foster is the founder of Jumping Beans, a New Zealand-based preschool gym programme that teaches very small children physical literacy. She extended my understanding of the importance of developing children's physical abilities.

Several studies link physical activity with academic learning, highlighting the importance of movement as the foundation of learning. Pre-schoolers taught how to climb, roll and tumble learn the building blocks for many other aspects of development, building brain pathways as they play.

Benefits of developing physical literacy:

- Tiny children learn to control their bodies through learning fundamental movement patterns such as locomotion, springing and landing, and manipulative skills like ball throwing and catching.
- They learn how to safely engage with others; to take turns and to be part of a team.

- It teaches the children skills that help minimise accidents – a form of future-proofing, if you like.
- It builds parental confidence to let them engage in healthy rough-and-tumble, instead of falling into the modern trap of cocooning and cotton-wool wrapping their children.
- Even more importantly, it also builds resilience and self-control.

Consider this

It might not be an overnight hike, and it might not be a developmental programme such as Jumping Beans, but how much time do your children spend playing outside? It's relatively easy for country children to be active outside, but many town children spend inordinate amounts of time glued to technology.

Keep them active – outside where possible. It's healthy and they'll learn far more.

See also:

Lesson 6: *Don't mollycoddle them – kids need to learn resilience and self-control*

Lesson 66: *A creative way for technology to be your friend*

Lesson 67: *How is screen time impacting your children?*

Resource Section: *Article by Jamie Morton. 'Obesity study asks if under-5s active enough'*

LESSON 5:

Boys need challenges - take the wraps off your sons

A chance conversation with my friend George about kayaking opened my eyes to a distinction about males that, as a mother of five sons and a grandmother of eleven boys, you'd think I would have worked out years ago.

'*Does your wife kayak with you?*' I'd asked George, who had recently remarried. '*No, and I haven't encouraged her to,*' he replied, to my surprise.

'*I've been teaching kayaking for many years,*' he explained. '*It's really made me appreciate the differences between men and women.*

'*What I've learnt is that when you teach a group of girls or women to do something with a high risk factor, with few exceptions their underlying motivation is to learn how to manage it safely.*

For instance, most don't enjoy having to tip out under the water and wait 20 seconds before kicking loose from their kayak and rising to the surface. I've noticed that almost all females are motivated away from risk and toward safety and security.

'*The majority of males, on the other hand, are motivated towards challenge and away from comfort and security. It's an innate testosterone drive – not something that's learned.*

'*Once a kayak class graduates from the beginner programme and starts to paddle in open water the guys will almost always turn even a social paddle into a competition, either against each other or against their own performance. Almost all will also seek tough new challenges. A typical group of women don't seek competition to anything like the same degree. Most of them will choose to paddle with others, enjoying the combination of socialising, exercise and scenery.*

'*Of course my wife and I could enjoy social kayaking. But she's not *that interested in the sport and definitely wouldn't enjoy the competitive and adventurous style of kayaking I love most. So I save that particular activity for when I can go hard out. We do other things together.'*

I've thought a lot about George's comments since then. It seems to me that our job as parents of boys is to grow responsible mature young men. Perhaps if we are at least aware of the basic need of boys to push boundaries, we'll enjoy the raising of them even more.

For women, it takes a different and special kind of courage to let go, to allow our boys the space to stumble and hurt themselves, to not restrict them unnecessarily. These days many women raise their sons without a full-time father figure in the home, as I did for some years. Most teachers of primary school children are women. Do we unconsciously try to restrict our boys in our desire to keep them safe? Do we unconsciously try to make them behave in ways that are comfortable and socially acceptable to women? Looking back I'm sure I did. The rough-house rumbles in the lounge, the farting, belching and peeing competitions …. do other mothers also recall feeling bewildered and wondering which planet their kids came from?

In hindsight, perhaps my boys were lucky there were so many of them, that they spent large amounts of time with their father, and that my ineffectual attempts to soften and civilise family activities were watered down! Adventurous lives are a signature note in our family, and the next generation is being brought up the same way.

LESSON 6:

Don't mollycoddle them – kids need to learn resilience and self-control

Why we must let them learn self-control

A very interesting longitudinal study led by Professor Richie Poulton has been running in New Zealand since 1972. Under the umbrella of the University of Otago, the Dunedin Multidisciplinary Health & Development Study (Dunedin Study for short) embarked on a ground-breaking nature/nurture test, to study 1037 babies for their entire lives. In 2016, they were still tracking at 95% retention. Their research assesses many criteria, of which one is self-control.

One set of findings, run when the participants were 32, showed clear evidence that the children with higher self-control skills as very small children are having significantly fewer issues with crime, drugs, and educational problems of both learning and behaviour. The skills include conscientiousness, self-discipline and perseverance. The participants with the highest quotas of self-control have shown to be more effective with health, financial literacy and wealth creation, relationships and contentment. Link this to the work of organisations like Jumping Beans and we immediately see simple, fun ways to encourage the development of self-control.

If you've got boys it's even more important to extend them

'Boys Adrift: the five factors driving the growing epidemic of unmotivated boys and underachieving young men' by Leonard Sax M.D., Ph.D. is a 'must read'. You'll find practical and useful

insights into what current trends in education are doing to many boys; such as the impact of video games on their behaviour. Also, his theories on why there's such a rapid increase in ADHD, and what can be done about it, and how plastics are affecting male hormone levels, and much more.

Just one of the points Dr Sax develops is that many schools (at least in America) have all but eliminated opportunities for kids to develop resilience through experiencing true competition in their physical education programmes. The rationale seems to be that if a child doesn't win at whatever they're competing in, that their self-esteem might be damaged; therefore it's better that no one be a 'loser'. But if we agree with George's comment in Lesson 5, isn't it critical to provide healthy opportunities for our boys to flex their muscles, prove their manliness and learn to handle competition and frustration? Certainly Dr Sax believes so as well.

We also see this 'softening of potential hurt' on an academic level. Look at the modern exam systems. Heaven forbid that a young adult might feel 'dumb' when they don't get good enough grades! But here's the rub: in the adult world, you're a responsible worker – or you lose your job. If you're a commission agent you have to make sales – or you don't eat. If you're in finance, the accounts are either correct – or they're not. If you run your own business, you either succeed or you don't. Real life isn't one of half measures. If we don't give our children the chance to learn that lesson when we're there to support them, we do them great harm. The real world doesn't soft-soap failure and incompetence. Failure is failure. Let's stop this PC nonsense!

LESSON 7:

The 'zero tolerance to violence' trend has gone way too far

Another area Sax discusses is the trend towards 'zero tolerance to violence'. In some schools this means students are punished for writing violent stories and small children are penalised for turning sticks or pieces of paper into guns. Some years ago our family had a brush with the same kind of thinking.

Four of my grandchildren lived for two years on a very large army base in mid-Victoria, Australia. Their dad had made them a wooden toy gun each – after all, guns are part of their normal life. Out in the scrub, playing with their mates, their homemade wooden guns were the envy of all their buddies. This was reported back to Dad, the 'arms manufacturer'.

'Well', he said, *'if you want to make a bit of pocket money your mum and I will help you make some for sale. Ask your friends if they'll pay $11.50 for a gun like yours.'* (Teaching the two older boys responsibility and commitment was the real focus; the product was just a vehicle.)

And so began an entrepreneurial business for the eight and ten-year-olds, helped by Mum and Dad on the machine end of production. (Skill-saws really were a tad dangerous!) Orders came flooding in, different models were designed and the boys learnt to sandpaper and paint; to manage orders, deliveries and money. Even the neighbourhood girls got in on the act – hot items were the made-to-order pink AK47s. (Soldier Dad cringed but *'the customer is always right'*.)

The first stall at the local on-base market generated $147 for the lads. Excited by their business success the boys got Mum to apply for a stall at a nearby town's Saturday market.

However, that plan was knocked back when the woman

on the end of the phone said, very heatedly, *'No way can your children sell wooden guns at our market. We don't allow anything that encourages violence.'*

I was telling the story to a very experienced kindergarten teacher. She gave a wry laugh.

'You can't stop boys playing with guns. They're hard-wired that way. Many times I've seen children, brought up by pacifist parents who've completely protected their children from any violent influences, pick up a stick and turn it into a gun. How on earth do we think we can change millennia of male protector/hunter/provider instincts?'

Let's work *with* nature, not against it. Turn off the TV and video games with their far more aggressive, unreal and 'consequence-free' violence and let the children act out their natural instincts in healthy outdoor play. If they hurt themselves, they'll learn.

Young entrepreneurs

LESSON 8:

Get those kids out of cars!

My buddy Alison and I were doing our usual morning exercise – flapping our gums as well as our shoes. A brisk 40-minute walk down nearby country roads was our normal route, with wide-ranging conversation as a bonus kick-start for the day.

A car zipped past. I casually noticed a school uniform in the passenger seat. About two minutes later the same car returned, now just carrying Mum. As we turned out of the short road we'd been walking on, another car pulled up, disgorged a couple of pre-teens at the bus stop, backed around and also went back home.

Nothing unusual in this, you'd say? No, and that's the point. It's such a common occurrence in both town and country that most of us never even think about it.

Let me paint the scene a little more. The cars had come from two short country no-exit roads to the junction with the main road, a pick-up point for the school bus. Neither of these roads have much traffic, one has a footpath some of the way and both have clear visibility and plenty of space to safely walk. It's a very quiet rural and small-holding country setting; safety is not an issue.

Let's step away from kids going to school for a moment and think a bit wider. Do any of these issues concern you?

- The increase in children as well as adults suffering from obesity-related disease.
- Young people who don't take responsibility.
- Young people with limited commonsense, maturity and resilience in unexpected situations.

- Too much to do and a feeling that there's never enough time.
- The increasingly frenetic pace of life.
- People who expect to be entertained rather than making their own fun.
- The price of fuel.
- Pollution of our environment.
- Congestion on the roads, especially during school and university terms.

My real question is: why do parents think they do their kids a favour by driving them everywhere? Think about the list above. If children had to get out of bed a bit earlier, stretch their legs and walk down the road to the nearest bus, or bike or walk to school; if they had to suffer the consequences of dawdling, of missing the bus, what would happen?

- Would it give the kids exercise?
- Would it be good for their health?
- If parents said, 'Out the door' instead of dropping their work to run them down the road, would it save that busy parent a little bit of time in each day?
- Would it save fuel and vehicle expenses?
- Would it reduce pollution a little?

… and we could go on. I'm sure you get the picture.

The fastest way to do something, to get somewhere, isn't necessarily the best way

A week after the school transport scene just described, I was travelling through the stunningly beautiful South Island of New Zealand, on a speaking tour. The road took me from rolling pastoral mid-Canterbury through snow-covered mountain passes, past the jewels of Lakes Tekapo and Pukaki, past Mount Cook and down to the lakeside town of Wanaka. The glorious snow-covered peaks drew my eyes to the brilliant clear blue sky. As my eyes lifted, my soul soared. (If you're a *Lord of the Rings* fan you've seen some of this scenery.) *'How truly blessed I am to have this opportunity,'* I thought.

Two days later I was in a plane, winging my way home to the north. From my window I had a brilliant view of the snow-blanketed jagged backbone and ribs running the length of the South Island. Did my soul soar? Yes, but nothing like two days prior when I was in the midst of it, touching the snow, listening to the birds, observing the detail. Of course, it's faster to fly and often we have to – but sometimes the best way is not the fastest way.

What does this have to do with kids taking responsibility for getting themselves to school under their own steam? Everything, I believe.

- As they kick down the road to school or take the bus they become more aware of their environment. They'll see things in gardens and roadsides (and paddocks if they're country children).
- Children are naturally curious – it gives them the chance to explore instead of stunting their curiosity with man-made limitations.
- They have to refine social skills if they walk with other children. (I remember some fierce arguments with my older cousins as I walked two miles to the bus along country roads as an eight year old, but it taught us a lot about how to get along.)
- They'll have their safety-first road knowledge sharpened through daily use.
- They learn to take responsibility for their own time-keeping. If they miss the bus or get to school late they have to explain why to both parents and teachers, and suffer the consequences.
- If they get wet they quickly learn that raincoats are not just a nuisance.

- Could they get into trouble? Sure. That's how they learn.
- Could there be danger? We've got to let our kids learn that too. Packing them with cotton wool isn't the way to teach them anything.

Some ideas on how to keep them safe

- Teach them the safety rules and then trust them to be the smart children you know you've raised.
- When they're little, walk or cycle with them.
- Or, get an older child to walk or ride with them.
- Start a walking bus in your community if they're young.

Over-protecting our children is not loving them; instead, it hurts them. We all benefit from being stretched, no matter what our age.

LESSON 9:

Parenting for maturity and independence

The following contribution is from the blog of my friend Karen Boyes. Her work is almost exclusively with schools and students.

Whilst on holiday, tragedy struck the young girl next door... her mother died. It was unexpected. She had been unwell and the hospital wanted to do an urgent scan and had scheduled it for the following week. She died before that day. The young girl, I'll call her Claire, is 10 years old and an only child. She is my daughter's holiday play friend. We often holiday in the same spot and the girls have been holiday 'mates' for many years.

What struck me about this horrible tragedy was the lack of independence Claire has. Living only a few doors from the school gates, her Mum had walked her to and from school every day; every single day of her five years of school. It really got me thinking. I know far too many parents who do everything for their children. I know many children who do not know how to do simple tasks.

Now I'm not suggesting parents plan for an early departure. However, we do have a responsibility to help our children develop into independent and mature citizens who are ready to leave home when the time is right. I saw a quote once that said: 'When your children don't need you anymore, you have done a great job.' There will always be times we need or want our parents for support, guidance or companionship. I believe the quote is about independence; about being able to do everyday tasks, at age-appropriate stages, on their own.

It starts early with small steps – having children help you with the daily tasks. Tasks might take longer; they may even mess it up. This is all part of the very important learning process.

If your children are older, it is not too late. Chat about the importance of working together as a family, sharing the load, preparing for adulthood.

Make it fun. Wear cleaning aprons and scarves if it helps. Put on some fun music. Use a timer and small incentives if needed. My teens still love the ice cream challenge! They have 60 minutes to clean their rooms (photographs of what their tidy room looks like are on the inside of their wardrobe doors – including under the bed and the wardrobe floor.) If completed to my satisfaction, we go out and buy an ice cream each.

As a parent, you may need to let go of perfectionism – they will make mistakes. They will not do it to your level of skill – they are still learning. Your child did not get up and walk perfectly the first time either. It took encouraging words, affirmations, praise and a helping hand for them to learn to walk. The same is true of all learning and especially if being able to complete tasks independently is a goal. It requires you, as the parent, to be patient, flexible, nurturing, encouraging and forgiving.

It may require you to slow down, take more time. It is easy in our hurried busy world to think it is quicker and easier to do tasks yourself. If so, what do your children learn?

Start slow and ensure your child has mastered each task before you add the next. Some will take longer than others. Be kind and teach them how to do the job correctly. Sweeping the front step by moving the dirt from one side to the other is not OK. It means removing the dirt. They may not stack the dishwasher exactly as you like it; breathe, walk away and leave it – the dishes will still get clean. (If not, you now have a learning point for next time.)

Instructions posted nearby save the huffing and puffing of 'I don't know how to do it!'

> **Washing machine Instructions**
> ───────────────
> 1. Press powder ①
> 2. Choose wash cycle
>   – usually regular
> 3. Select wash temp – cold
> 4. Select water level – auto
> 5. Select spin speed – fast
> 6. Add powder
>   – full load = 1/2 scoop
> 7. Press Start ▶||

In our home, if the children want special snacks in their lunch, they have to make them. Last night both were in the kitchen making cupcakes! Our 16-year-old son is an expert banana cake maker.

The fruits of your efforts will pay off. Recently my husband and I realised neither of us would be home to cook dinner and we simply rang the children and asked them to cook the meal. It was on the table when we got home. A healthy, hot meal. It is all about helping out and ensuring they can live independently one day

As I am writing this, I called out to my son to please empty the dishwasher and I'll stack it. He jumped up and did it immediately – not because he is perfect – but because he has learned if he gets on with it quickly, he can go back to doing what he really wants. A great life lesson.

Praise all efforts and be sure to have your child overhear you telling someone how helpful and independent they are becoming. When children 'eavesdrop' on a compliment, the positive vibes are felt deeper within.

Still not sure? Maybe this statistic will help scare some into action – the average age of a child leaving home is 27... yes twenty seven! Are you still going to be doing their laundry, cleaning up their messes, cooking their food at 27?

Still not convinced? This is one of my favourite graphics!

[reprinted with permission from Karen Boyes, Spectrum Education
www.spectrumeducation.com/parenting]

See also:

Section VII: *Raising teenagers without pulling your hair out*

LESSON 10:

Shifting boundaries

Sometimes it's very challenging to know what boundaries to set. For example, by the time our oldest son Chris began school we had drilled into him the importance of not hitting other kids. At the first parent/teacher meeting that well-intentioned boundary was tipped on its ear, at least outside the home. His teacher said, *'Chris is a lovely little boy, but unfortunately he's too gentle. I'm afraid we're in the real world here: he's getting bullied by Jason. I can't say it, but please would you tell him that if Jason thumps him, he's allowed to thump him back.'*

It was rather a shock to his idealistic parents, but we passed the message on.

The family often has a chuckle about it now – that pacifist kid went into the army and for years a significant part of his work has been dealing with international bullies and terrorists! Do we thank Miss Cavanagh, I wonder?

We start out with values and beliefs that have stood us in good stead up until this major life change called parenting. Many times they will hold true for the new role. But, be prepared to continually evaluate and adjust if necessary. Very little in life is totally black and white.

In my experience there is never only one way of doing things, or of living life. Unexpected turns in the road are part of our journey – and parenting is no exception.

LESSON 11:

Reward the behaviour you want more of – praise is your tool

Whatever we focus on enlarges. Praise your children when they perform well and minimise your attention on activities you don't want them to focus on, or behaviour you'd prefer them not to engage in. Praise releases energy, criticism kills it.

I went through a very frustrating stage with son James when he was nine. Every time I asked him to do some perfectly innocuous task, all I got in return was moans and complaints. Refrains like: *'It's not fair; it's Maurice's turn; I didn't make the mess; I don't want to,'* echoed around the house. In the midst of my frustration, one day I realised I had begun to sound as cranky as him.

At the end of my tether, one day I remembered learning about Positive Parenting. In a nutshell, if you reinforce the desired behaviour and ignore or give as little attention as possible to *unsatisfactory* behaviour, the bad behaviour is supposed to diminish. I was clear out of ideas so decided to give it a go.

I picked a calm moment. *'Jimmy, I'm not happy about the way you complain every time you're asked to do a chore. And I'm not happy about myself either – I'm beginning to sound like you when I growl at your grizzles!*

'I've had a better idea. Every time I catch you not *grizzling when you're asked to do something, you'll get a tick. We'll keep a list on the fridge. When you've earned 10 ticks, you get an ice cream. And if I forget to notice that you haven't complained, you're allowed to remind me, so we can get those ticks up there as fast as possible.'*

Jimmy took up the suggestion enthusiastically. I remembered to praise him to the skies the first few times he willingly accepted a task, and amazingly quickly the habit became reinforced. After three ice creams we forgot to keep track and it was never an issue again.

LESSON 12:

Mean what you say – and follow through

If we tell our children that a certain action will have a certain punishment, don't weaken. Stick to it – they *will* always test us. A threat not carried through is worse than wasted words; it teaches them to ignore your requests.

For example: *'Clean up your room before you leave for school in the morning. Anything left lying around will be thrown out and you won't see it again.'*

The first time you might put left-around gear in the garage just to give them a shock. The next time, give it to the Salvation Army. I've known others to throw clothing, music, shoes or favourite toys out the window – wet or shine.

Case study: The 24-hour box

Catherine attended one of my talks. She's a mother of five, a dairy farmer, a part-time teacher and also much involved with community activities.

'I got sick of tidying up after my children so I decided to start a 24-hour box. The deal is, if I find anything lying around it goes in the box. After 24 hours, if no-one has claimed it and put it away, the 'abandoned' property goes in the rubbish.

'Once the system was fully in place, only a few precious items had to be thrown out before the lesson stuck. Now everyone takes responsibility for their 'stuff' and the house stays pretty tidy.'

LESSON 13:

If they damage something, they pay

One rainy weekend all the children were playing in the lounge. It was during my really broke single-parent days and every penny was needed in four places. Eldest son Chris, who was about 13, was idly kicking a football around the furniture.

'Chris, if you want to kick that ball, take it outside. Continue as you are and you'll break the window. And if you do, you'll pay for the repair.'

You can tell where this story is going, can't you!

He ignored me and a few minutes later, sure enough, one of the smaller windows was broken. (Lucky for him, it wasn't the big picture window!)

'OK, you were warned. The next time you get paid (he earned money by doing chores for his farming father) *you will pay for this.'*

The window was fixed, the bill came in, and Chris was informed of the extent of his debt.

A few weeks later I heard him say to one of his siblings: *'I'm going to buy .... for Cathy's birthday with my next pay.'*

'Oh no, you're not,' was my quick reply. *'You're going to pay off that broken window first. Debts and obligations first, then the fun stuff, even if it's something nice for someone else.'*

Somewhat grumpily he handed over the money.

The consequences? All the younger ones were party to the conversation and no one ever after tried to dodge their fiscal responsibilities. And this same son became very responsible about his money and a very good saver. He bought his first rental property when he was only 19 and on a lowly second lieutenant's salary, his first year out of Officer Cadet School.

LESSON 14:

What is good discipline?

Have you ever noticed this seeming contradiction: very loving, caring mums and dads whose children are a mobile disaster area? They cause their poor parents endless grief and struggle, suck their energy and leave a storm of distress and wasted time and money in their wake.

Case study 1

My friend Jan took far too many calls from head-masters to explain why Richard was yet again suspended or expelled. She had to call the police when she found stolen property in his bedroom. Eventually she learnt to apply tough love and changed the locks to keep an older Richard and his druggie friends out of her house. What could have gone wrong? He'd been such a cute kid.

Case study 2

A couple who worked at the same university as me (before I started popping out babies) had four children. The word on campus was *'Take cover if the Cartwright children come into your building. They're horrors!'* The parents seemed blissfully unaware that their children were destructive ill-mannered brats whom no one wanted to deal with. I was bemused by this; the parents were well-educated, intelligent people who knew more about behaviour and communication than most. I figured it had to be something to do with their much-discussed permissive parenting practices.

In years to come, every time I let my kids get away with poor behaviour, I worried about whether I was turning them into

Cartwright-type monsters.

So what was the answer, I began to ask myself? As humans, we're comfort seekers. Surely we're not meant to deny ourselves and our children some of the finer things of life that we've struggled to earn? Was there a magic formula here that I was missing? Was there a middle road?

From this end of the child-raising continuum, I've realised there isn't just one answer to the apparent mystery of why some really good people end up with very challenging children. However, there is one core lesson I know to be pure gold. Although the ways of fulfilling our parenting responsibilities change as the children grow, the confidence to lovingly but firmly hold true to your standards, despite the masterful manipulation of juvenile 'terrorists', is essential to being an effective parent.

In following lessons you'll find some suggestions and ideas which might help.

LESSON 15:

How to end 'spoilt brat' syndrome

It wasn't until my children were all grown up that I found a comprehensive answer to the questions raised above. It was late 2005 and I was waiting at a tube station in London when a book review in The Times caught my eye with its catchy title: *How to end spoilt brat syndrome.*

Back home it took me a while to track down the book being reviewed, *The Pampered Child Syndrome: how to recognize it, how to manage it, and how to avoid it – a guide for parents and professionals.*

Author Maggie Mamen is a Canadian psychologist who works extensively with children and parents. In a compassionate and very practical way she not only paints the problems but also shares solutions and guidance.

As I read it, I became really excited. I'm so glad I made the effort to find the book – not only is it easy to read and eminently practical, but it addressed the muddle of questions that had traipsed their muddy feet through my child-raising years.

Here's my summary of some of Mamen's points:

- *Our job as parents is to fit our children for the world outside home. It's a 16-20 year project you sign on for when you create a baby. Play now – pay later!*
- *Life isn't perfect – if we cocoon our kids, we weaken them.*
- *Why we must let our children learn how to deal with unhappiness, rather than back away from it.*
- *Ideas on how to safely allow our children space to experience the discomfort that's part of life.*
- *Think of family life like a management team. If we own a company*

we don't allow our junior staff members to dictate the policies and financial management of the firm. Good bosses will often consider the needs and opinions of their junior team members, but it's typically business suicide to allow those same people to make long term decisions. They have neither the maturity and business experience, nor the ultimate responsibility, for the results.

- *Parents are the bosses; we abdicate the role at our peril, thereby hurting our children.*
- *If we don't teach our children right, if we abdicate our responsibilities as authoritative parents (using the authority vested in us), if we don't own and apply our job description, we'll pay for much longer – through unhappiness, disharmony, anger, grief, alcohol and drug abuse, and in many cases ultimately in the courts.*
- *Child-centred parenting is back-to-front. The kids don't know enough, nor do they have the maturity, to make appropriate decisions. As parents, of course we should talk to and listen to our children but not to the exclusion of practical adult common sense.*
- *Many of the most troubled parents have been seduced by child-focused philosophies that sound reasonable, such as 'involve the child/ren in all family discussions; give them everything; make sure they want for nothing; allow them to choose their own food, bed-time, hours of homework, activities from a young age; and don't insist they do things they don't want to do.'*

LESSON 16:

What we say and what children hear are rarely the same thing

I've noticed, and Maggie Mamen discusses this point in some depth, that the words we use can make a profound difference to our results with our children. Unfortunately, what the adults say and what their children hear are not the same thing. Consequences are almost always unpleasant.

It happens even between intelligent and well educated adults so this shouldn't come as any surprise, but check out Mamen's list below.

What we say	vs	What children hear
We want our children to be happy and comfortable.	=	When I experience loss or failure, or feel sad, upset, frustrated or disappointed, someone should make me feel better.
We want our children to be stimulated and enriched.	=	I should never be bored. I should only be asked to do things that are stimulating and enriching, not things that are tedious and boring. In fact, if it's not interesting, I won't do it.
We want our children to make their own choices.	=	No one should tell me what to do; I should be allowed to make up my own mind.
We want our children to be included in family decisions.	=	Adults should not make any decisions without consulting me first. I should be part of the management team.

We want our children to be given reasons for things that they are asked to do.	=	I will not do anything unless you give me a reason why I should. It must be a good reason. If I don't agree with the reason, you have to keep looking to find one that I do agree with.
We want our children to be treated equally and fairly.	=	I should be treated the same as adults. If other people can do it, I should be able to do it too.
We want our children to express their feelings and be heard.	=	I should never do anything unless I feel like doing it. Are you listening? Did you not hear what I said?
We want our children to have positive self-esteem.	=	I should always feel good about myself.

© *Reproduced by permission. Mamen, Maggie. The Pampered Child Syndrome: How to Recognize it, How to Manage it, and How to Avoid it - A Guide for Parents and Professionals. Jessica Kingsley Publishers, London. 2005, rev.ed. 2006.*

I closed Mamen's book with a sense of elation. At last I'd found someone who explained the mystery of good parents with badly behaved children. Looking back, there was a sense of relief. Despite all those topsy-turvy child-raising years and an often dysfunctional marriage, we did get the most important things right – one of them being consistency with discipline and standards.

It was also encouraging to read that poor beginnings can be turned around and a healthy family can be recreated, providing the parents involved are prepared to do something about it. In almost all cases, with the right adult guidance even difficult children can become healthy well-adjusted adults and productive members of society. (If you'd like more specifics, get the book. I wouldn't do Mamen's techniques justice by summarising further in this short commentary.)

If you're in the same place as I was over 35 years ago, be reassured. It's OK to be the boss of your children – that's what parents need to be, if they're doing their job right. Children get their turn when they grow up but for the first 16 years, whether we like it or not, the buck stops with us. Abdication of our responsibility to be authoritative parents comes at great long-term cost and grief.

'No' is a love word

LESSON 17:

The consequences of child-centred upbringing

Let's pick up one point from the previous two lessons, regarding child-centred parenting. It sounds good and reasonable – or does it? After all, anything child-centred must be OK, wouldn't you suppose?

To paraphrase Jesse Owens, the great Black American runner of the 1936 Berlin Olympics: When our children are little, of course we protect them from harm. But as soon as they're big enough to face the consequences of their actions without danger, if we love them we have to let them feel any associated hurt and pain they've caused. If we jump in to smooth things out, if we try to protect them and take away their pain, we weaken them. We actually hurt them by not allowing them to develop the skills necessary to live in the real world.

Case study 1: 'We don't want the children to want for anything'

Vince and his sisters grew up in a very loving and protective family. Their parents' focus was always to provide everything the children wanted. Their mother made it her life's work to shelter and support them. Their father worked very hard to earn a good income and set up family trusts so they would never, even as adults, experience the hardships he and their mother had experienced as young people. The parents have now passed on and today their children are in their forties.

Of course they've all got some good traits but – they're toxic to the people close to them. Their issues include: severe instability with employment; emotional abuse of work colleagues, partners and children; tantrums when things don't go their way; breakups with partners who won't do what they want. Coincidence? I don't think so.

They also carry an *It's not fair* or *Poor me* attitude into the world. They have low resilience and a limited ability to work through life's problems.

Do you know people like this? A friend of mine had the misfortune to be married to Vince for 10 years. It took her at least as many years to recover from the emotional abuse he threw at her.

Case study 2: The cost of cocooning

Phillip and his two sisters had a different situation. When they were children, their father was very authoritarian and distant in his relationships with all his children, but especially with Phillip. (Definition of authoritarian: 'demanding absolute and unquestioning obedience'). He loved them but didn't – perhaps couldn't – show it.

Their very loving mother tried to compensate for her husband's heavy-handed discipline, apparent indifference and lack of affection by trying to make things easier for her children. She did everything in her power to take the rough edges off the rejections, tried to provide the love they sought from their dad, constantly looked for ways to make life easier for them. She put enormous energy into cocooning them from the results of their father's behaviour.

Nothing wrong with that, you'd think. She was a wonderful woman, but sadly her kindness made life even harder for her offspring; she went too far. For instance, you'd often hear her say things like, *'You poor thing. Let me do that for you.'* She willingly carried the load for them, leaving them to run off and play. More often than not, they weren't made to take responsibility – she could be relied upon to pick up the slack behind them.

Phillip grew into a lazy adult. For example, before he married he used to save up his washing until there was nothing left to wear (with a lot of work clothes this could take three weeks). Red Letter days were the frequent visits by his mother to his bachelor abode. She'd spend the first two days slaving away, getting his enormous pile of stinky labourer's clothes all clean and back in the drawers. When he came in from his work day he'd sit around talking to her, instead of helping. You won't be surprised to hear that he carried that behaviour into his marriage – after all, a woman's role was to run around after his needs and desires (wasn't it?). No surprise that the marriage didn't survive!

The older sister had reasonable self-esteem and her problems were less severe, perhaps because she was her father's favourite.

However, the younger sister struggled all her life with primary relationships, money, alcohol, depression and self-esteem issues.

What happened here? In both true-life examples the parents were good people. Unfortunately they didn't prepare their children for the real world.

LESSON 18:

Share the load

In today's business world, where so many parents do double duty – working in the commercial world and also running a home and family – it's more important than ever for everyone's wellbeing that all family members contribute to chores and childcare duties. A lot of tasks can be done by the children.

Quite apart from taking unfair pressure and expectations off the ever-stretched parents (and some women still carry an inequitable portion of domestic responsibility), there are a couple of other equally important reasons.

Parents, it's your job to raise boys who pull their weight around the house

As we raised the six children, right from a very young age our one daughter loved helping her mum with housework. (No, I *guarantee* I didn't try to mould her that way!) On the other hand, the five boys were your regular reluctant starters when it came to chores.

I determined early in my child-raising years that my sons would be considerate and helpful men. Girlfriends, if your partner isn't much of a home helper, it's your job to break what is often an inter-generational pattern.

Many a time, as they grizzled and complained about their chores, I'd say, *'One day your wives will thank me!'* They do! The boys have grown into great dads and thoughtful husbands. And now, four of my five daughters, one created and four acquired, have the same task with their composite collection of 11 boys! The fifth family has all girls and their dad is a great role model

– he loves to cook and is very involved with all aspects of the domestic routines.

Children need to learn to take responsibility from a very young age

If kids are allowed to get away with not making their bed when instructed, not picking up their toys, not taking out the trash, if parents say things like *'I can't get them to do what they're told'* and then do their children's tasks, the bad habits of those children will carry into their adult lives.

Anyone who's worked with such people knows they act as though the world owes them a living. They seem to think that shoddy work is acceptable. They act as though others will automatically clean up after them. They're inconsiderate and sulky or surly when asked to re-do bad workmanship. And they're either incapable of forming healthy long-lasting relationships because they're so self-centred, or they form dysfunctional relationships with co-dependent partners who put up with their unacceptable behaviour.

LESSON 19:

What we can learn from the French about raising children

A few years ago I accompanied my daughter-in-law Lauren, her mother, and our shared granddaughters to France to attend the wedding of Lauren's host brother from her year as an exchange student. We experienced all the lovely things you'd expect – and I learnt a lot as well.

The French raise their children differently, and get markedly better behaviour than what I commonly see at home.

In all the visits I've made to France I cannot remember ever seeing a French child having a tantrum or acting up. And on the wedding visit I was with many children over the first 20 days, including at the wedding which, in true French style, was an awesome family event in multiple parts, at three different venues and spread over two days.

One example is mealtime. I've noticed quite young children patiently waiting for their *dîner* (dinner) which usually shows up about eight o'clock. Even toddlers are rarely fed earlier. It's regarded as important that they sit at the table with the grown-ups and learn to be part of the wider family group. Neither are they allowed to dominate the conversation, although they certainly are not repressed. Once they've eaten they politely ask to be excused and are allowed to go off to play – but not to watch TV (at least in the families I spent most time with).

However, it wasn't just mealtime that produced well-behaved French children. Everywhere I went I was impressed. How is it that their kids are consistently better behaved than many in Western English-speaking countries?

I found the key to this puzzle in my two-hour stop-over at Singapore on the way home. Browsing in a bookshop, I was halted in mid-stride by *Bringing Up Bébé – one American mother discovering the wisdom of French parenting* by Pamela Druckerman.

The journalist author has lived in Paris for some years. About to have her first baby, she began to notice the same thing I had; French children are different to American children. Here are some excerpts from the inside front cover:

- *French parents insist they're not doing anything special. Yet the French children Druckerman knows sleep through the night at two or three months, while children of her American friends take a year or more.*
- *French kids eat well-rounded meals that are more likely to include braised leeks than chicken nuggets.*
- *Her American friends spend their visits resolving spats between their kids, but her French friends sip coffee while the children play.*
- *French mothers assume that even good parents aren't at the constant service of their children and that there's no need to feel guilty about this. They have an easy, calm authority with their kids that Druckerman can only envy.*
- *French kids are just as boisterous, curious and creative as Americans. They're just far better behaved and more in command of themselves.*
- *French parents are extremely strict about some things, and strikingly permissive about others. To be a different kind of parent, you don't just need a different parenting philosophy.* **You need a very different view of what a child actually is.**

One theme she constantly comes back to is teaching them delayed gratification. She asks:

'Could it be that making children delay gratification – as middle-class French parents do – actually makes them calmer and more resilient? Whereas middle-class American kids, who are in general more used to getting what they want right away, go to pieces under stress?'

'Whenever I go back to America, I realize that miserable, screaming toddlers demanding to get out of their strollers or pitching themselves *onto the sidewalk are part of the scenery of daily life.*

'I rarely see such scenes in Paris. French babies and toddlers, who are used to waiting longer, seem oddly calm about not getting what they want right away. When I visit French families and hang out with their kids, there's a conspicuous lack of whining and complaining.

'I regularly see what amounts to a minor miracle: adults in the company of small children at home, having entire cups of coffee and full-length adult conversations. Waiting is even part of the parenting vernacular. Instead of saying "quiet" or "stop" to rowdy kids, French parents often just issue a sharp "attend", which means "wait".'

She also observed a major focus on **teaching children their place** in the family and how to behave. The common French philosophy is very similar to the points made by Maggie Mamen and referred to earlier.

- *We're the parents; they're kids.*
- *We're the bosses; they need (and intuitively seek) boundaries.*
- *Our job is to teach them how to grow into well-adjusted members of society; their job is to be taught, with as little stress as possible to all concerned.*
- *There's no way they know what's good for themselves – and this applies to teenagers as well as toddlers.*

It seems to me that too many parents in today's over-informed and excessively politically correct world think their job is to make life smooth and easy for their little ones – smooth out the bumps, not let them get upset, or leave them upset for as short a time as possible. This includes not letting them feel too much frustration.

French parents, on the other hand, know that initial frustration (not getting what they want, when they want it) teaches children resilience, adaptability, patience and all the other good virtues that a well-adjusted adult would exhibit. It also makes life much less stressful for their families as they grow up – and it's never too early to start. It's really important for them to hear *'no'* and *'wait'*.

Badly behaved children seek boundaries. Give them guidelines and consequences, delivered clearly and firmly by the responsible adult, and they'll calm down very quickly. Every child will push the boundaries, and strong-willed children will push even more. If we as parents don't stand firm, we deny them the boundaries they seek – so they'll continue to push until they get them.

There's another key French national characteristic that applies to everyone, not just children, and that's a huge emphasis on good manners. Even small children are expected to be courteous, greet people with 'Bonjour' or 'Bonsoir' and at least two kisses (if they're family friends).

As a footnote to this point on good manners, you might be wondering about the arrogant Parisian shopkeepers you've heard of.

If we get rudeness it's almost always because we've (unintentionally) invited it. In many cases, especially with small businesses, you're actually entering their homes, albeit the commercial part. Because of this, a basic courtesy when you enter a French shop is to immediately greet the attendant. Consider our normal shopping behaviour in many Western countries; most of us don't greet the attendant until we're ready to purchase. So you can see why French shopkeepers think we're rude, and treat us accordingly.

Here's to more cultural exchanges. They help create a better informed and more tolerant world – if we take the time to listen, watch and learn.

Crepes in Brittany

SECTION II
TOP-LEVEL HABITS FOR BETTER FAMILY-TIME EFFECTIVENESS

LESSON 20:

Two life-changing habits

Two simple but life-changing habits are relevant to everything we do. If we don't teach them to our children they'll either struggle through life or they will be forced by circumstances to learn them the hard way.

1. The habit of momentum
2. The habit of completion

How do we build or capitalise on momentum?

When you're driving, think of how much faster you go through a set of lights if your wheels are still turning when the light turns green than if you're stationery when it changes.

It's easier to keep going on any activity when you're doing other similar tasks. Whether it's phone calls, emails, filing or other paperwork, it's faster and more efficient to batch or chunk similar activities than to chop and change constantly.

And what about completion?

Putting things away as you finish with them or at the next natural break is a simple and very visible example of the habit of completion. However, many people find this really powerful success habit a struggle.

When something else is demanding your attention, you've got someone waiting, or you're about to dash out the door to an appointment, it's easy to tell yourself *'I'll get back to that later'*, and move on to the new activity. The bulk of the old task is completed or taken as far as it needs to go. All that's left is to put things away to their final destinations. The pressure is off.

The new activity is more interesting, or more urgent. The natural thing is to want to move forward.

But there is a better way. Here's a personal experience to illustrate it.

I spent years learning to finish things. Until I *did* learn it, life seemed to be one long disorganised roller-coaster. I lurched from task to task with nothing ever quite completed. Occasionally I'd step back objectively and notice that a task was about 90-95% done, but the feeling of satisfaction for a job well done often eluded me. I finally noticed it was because items were often not put away at the end of an activity, or a small part was left undone. I lived in a tension of nothing-is-quite-finished. As most of us have experienced, a sense of incompletion compounds stress and makes us feel like there's just too much to do. The common result is overwhelm.

Even after becoming a time-management specialist I still had moments where the old habits would sneak up and I'd find myself in another pickle. One day there was a breakthrough. I'd been working on a big task; at the finish a large number of files were strewn all over the large office table. With an appointment looming, I thought I didn't have time to put them all away before going out.

A little voice in my head said, *'Robyn, do it now. It won't take long.'* Reluctantly at first, I started.

The momentum quickly built. There was time urgency anyway, but to my surprise it took only a couple of minutes to throw the files together and place the boxes in the cupboard. Decisions were quick and easy to make. I'd just finished working with the papers and everything was top-of-mind.

Later, I returned from my appointment, my head full of the new work required. Walking in the door, I saw the clean, tidy table and felt a powerful surge of relief. I realised that, had the clean-up been delayed, it would have taken much longer to sort later. The mess would probably have sat there for days, an invisible but very real mental burden, slowing down the creativity required for the next task.

Now, as soon as a task is finished, I immediately put the paperwork or item away if its destination is within arm's reach. If it's going to another part of the room, or another room, I make a pile and put it away at the next natural break. It takes only moments to return things when you've just been working on them, and your office (or home) always looks tidy.

LESSON 21:

The job is not done until everything is put away

Have you ever procrastinated on putting things away? Do your children do the same?

Let's take a closer look at the issue of momentum. Adults need to manage their own self-discipline to build the habit, but in most cases children need coaching and encouragement to excel.

If you're a parent who tends to leave things lying around, don't be surprised if your children follow your patterns. My mum had bad health when I was a teenager and although she was a stickler for cleanliness, tidiness was low on her priorities. As a result, I adopted her habits and had to work very hard as a young married woman to develop better methods.

The hardest part is the decision to act. Next time, as you stand there frozen with inertia, think back to the last time you *did* put things away quickly and how good it felt and looked.

Next time, when you and your children …

- Complete a task at work – put away tools and paperwork.
- Return from a trip – unpack everything immediately.
- Get out of bed – make it.
- Dress or undress – hang things up and put the dirty washing in the basket (or ready to go out the door when you next leave your bedroom).
- Eat something – clean up after yourself immediately, or as soon as you've eaten.
- Arrive home with used sports gear – clean and store it ready for next time.

- Finish a task in the garage, workshop or garden – clean down and put away the tools.

Last thoughts:

- Every piece of paper or equipment lying around is a symptom of a decision not made or an action not completed.
- Those struggling with space and clutter simply stop too soon – the job's not done until it's all put away. Just shift the finish line.
- Capitalise on your existing momentum. Do it now!

It's faster (and a lot easier) to shift a moving object than a stationary one!

LESSON 22:

How to teach the kids tidiness

Do you ever feel overwhelmed as you look at the mess of kids' toys and clothes spread around the house? You stand there, tired after a long day and just wish a genie would wave a magic wand – and then you realise you *are* the genie (or at least the kids think you are!)

The traditional answer is *'get the kids to put away after themselves'*. You might be thinking: *'But how? Isn't it easier to do it myself? I get tired of nagging them to put everything away.'*

For a permanent behaviour to become embedded, the entire family needs to consistently apply the core principles outlined below.

Case study 1

When they were aged from four to ten I spent a few days looking after my four oldest grandchildren.

The kids and I agreed that we'd give Mum a lovely surprise – we'd tidy up their rooms. To my amusement I noticed myself applying the same concepts I teach adults with messy offices.

- Let's pull everything out of the drawers and cupboards.
- We're going to put like with like.
- We'll make piles of 'same things' on the floor.
- Where do you think this should go? (for the older ones)
- Do you still use this?
- Whose is this?

- Now we'll put everything back. Which drawer would you like this in?
- 'System thinking, system thinking, guys!' (when something was hurled thoughtlessly back).

Sounds easy when you flick through a quick list of bullet points, doesn't it!

We made it fun. At the end of their one-on-one sessions each child had an immaculate wardrobe, drawers and floor – ready to surprise Mum. However, the next day the rubber really met the road, just as it does for grown-ups learning new habits. The only difference for adults is that they have to be their own stand-over man and make themselves accountable for keeping things tidy!

The habits need to be continually reinforced for them to stick. One session won't do it.

See also:

Karen Boyes' contribution at **Lesson 9:** *Parenting for maturity and independence.*

Case study 2

Some years ago I was called in to help a very creative Sydney family. Kay and her husband work from home as writers, movie and video makers and publicity, advertising and marketing consultants.

Their two-storey Lower North Shore bungalow was groaning under the weight of 'stuff'. In their small office, packed shelves rose almost to the high ceiling. It often housed three people and contained four computers, four desks, and an assortment of other cabinets. Over-flowing shelves lined the hall. In every room of the house piles of 'might be important' paperwork and/ or equipment was stuffed in filing drawers and cupboards, and heaped on tables, desks, shelves and floors.

The pair were under enormous stress. It felt as though they never had time to get to the really important and long-term projects or to make the money they knew they were capable of making. It was impossible to see the wood for the trees (transmuted into piles of paper!).

With a few slightly more sophisticated questions, but basically the same process as I used with the grandkids, we worked together for two days. I left them putting finishing touches to their transformed and efficient office, reluctant to stop. Excited and energised, they couldn't wait to start on the other rooms in the house.

The next morning Kay was on the phone to me. *'Our 13-year-old wants you to come and help him too. He's seen the transformation downstairs and he wants some of it!'*

Two hours later, principles explained as we went, a once-messy teenage bedroom was also transformed.

They continued the process after I left. It became an enormous clean-out of every part of the house. They took truckloads of junk to the dump, recycled a huge amount of 'treasure' to other destinations and pared back to only what they really needed and/or truly wanted to keep – for the right reasons, not because they were being hoarders. A few months later Kay wrote to tell me how their lives had been transformed.

I visited them about six years later and was very impressed to see that all three of them had maintained the process ever since.

Once you've felt the benefits, you just don't want to go back to the old mess. Success brings its own reward.

In both home and business these simple principles create an efficient working or living environment. When ignored, or not known, the outcome isstress and feelings of burnout and overload. So, start with the children. The habits of tidiness and momentum, once learnt and applied long enough to become routine, will have a huge impact on the rest of their lives.

See also:

Lesson 71: *Everyone's responsible for their own mess*

LESSON 23:

Don't be a perfectionist

Despite what I've just said above about teaching children to put away and be tidy, the early years will be anything but tidy. The best way to survive is to stay focused on what's important and forget perfectionism.

Do you have small people who leave marks on the furniture and windows or strew their toys all over the carpet and out in the yard? Does your entrance-way sometimes look like a second-hand all-sizes shoe shop?

Perhaps you hanker for a well-ordered and immaculate home; for calmness, orderliness, attractive space, everything efficient, things in their place and easy to find. That day will come – if you wish it – once they leave home. Until then, do the best you can, teach them to the best of your ability, but also go with the flow and enjoy each moment of joy.

The room may not be vacuumed and the windows may still need cleaning, but a quick tidy-up will keep the place looking presentable – and keep your own morale up!

A wise friend's advice

Many years ago, when the first four grandchildren were mostly pre-schoolers, a friend with a spotless home popped in for a coffee the day after the children had been to visit. I'd bustled around to tidy up but as we sat enjoying our coffee, I glanced over to the large picture window and gasped. The sun was pouring into the lounge and suddenly I noticed many sets of finger prints all over the lower reaches of the glass.

'Sorry the windows are so dirty,' I said. *'I had the grandchildren*

over yesterday.' They'd spent ages with noses pressed to the window, fascinated by the panoramic city view.

'*They are* **not** *dirty windows, Robyn,*' she replied. '*They're love marks.*'

Wear and tear, mess and dirt are indeed love marks.

The small children from the 'dirty windows' day are now teenagers with other interests and I'm not central to their lives any more. Make the most of those fast-flying years.

Andrea's tip: Be human!

I have a sign at the entrance door to our home: 'This house is clean enough to be healthy and dirty enough to be happy'. *I stick to that; no home needs to be clinical.*

Heather's tip: Forget perfect

Forget being perfect… happy is more important than tidy. Don't sweat the small stuff. Ask yourself: 'Will this matter in five years?' **Heather Douglas.**

LESSON 24:

Teach responsibility early

If your son has left his lunch at home, let him go hungry. He won't die from one missed meal. By not running to school with his lunch, you can bet he'll make darned sure he's got it tomorrow.

In my view, there's too much molly-coddling going on. Teachers everywhere talk about the number of hassled parents every day who show up with their child's lunch. Think about the time, energy and petrol wasted by the parent; the school secretary who has to stop what she's doing; the teacher whose class is interrupted.

Your children won't suffer serious consequences because they miss one meal – but the long-term consequences of learning responsibility will serve them well for the rest of their lives. Doing everything for your children does not benefit them in the long run; it simply robs them of the ability to plan and think for themselves.

Wasting time or investing time?

A further outcome of this 'mop up after the little darlings' behaviour is a huge but sometimes invisible waste of time. But it doesn't have to be this way.

A plug-the-gap action by you might take only a few minutes, which doesn't seem much at the time. Almost always it's quicker to run around after our children than leave them to do something at their speed; they're so much slower.

But – this isn't about saving time today. This isn't about making it easier for them (or us) today. Instead, it's about teaching them to be self-managing responsible adults – and that's our most important job, not just now but for the future.

Think about your workplace and the young people who work with you. Just consider how good it would be if every young employee started work with good time-management skills and an ingrained ethic of self-responsibility. It's our job as parents to get them there and it's never too soon to start.

A common lament is that some of today's young people seem to expect the world to be handed to them on a platter. We could go on at length talking about Gen X, Gen Y and any other Gen you like. However, it's not all bad. Many young people do know how to work hard, are wonderful to employ and don't exhibit the difficult behaviour we're being told to expect from them. Let's increase that number by teaching our children good habits at a young age.

Case study: I've left my swimming gear behind

It was my granddaughter Hannah's first day at school. For the previous year she'd watched her two older brothers catch the school bus to the nearby country school and she couldn't wait to join them.

Her mum offered to take her to and from school for the first few days. But Hannah was adamant; she would go on the bus – and she did.

Her two older brothers shepherded the excited birthday girl on and off the bus. She'd arrived at the gates of Nirvana with her large schoolbag – but – there was a problem. In her excitement Hannah had left her swim bag on the bus.

That afternoon, one disappointed small girl sat with the teacher on a hot summer's day, watching her classmates splash and frolic in the inviting water.

Should the bus driver have brought her swimming bag down to the school when he found it? Should the overworked teacher have run around to get Hannah's gear from the bus depot a few minutes' walk down the road? Should the teacher have rung

Mum to find it? And if she had, should Mum have dropped what she was doing to fetch and carry?

No to all of those, we think, and we're glad no-one tried to plug the gaps. Even though the family felt sad that Hannah's first day didn't go quite as smoothly as we would have liked, we totally agreed with her wise mother's comment: *'It's a good lesson. She'll be much more aware of her possessions now.'* It's no accident that she and her siblings have grown into very self-sufficient and independent young adults

Make a habit of running around after other people (of all ages), of sorting out their mistakes and minimising the consequences of their actions and you build an unfair expectation that this is the way it should be. It's kinder – if harder at first – to let them experience reality.

Now Hannah teaches her little cousin

LESSON 25:

Where possible synchronise activities or travel

For a time my oldest family of four grandchildren all went to the same indoor ice hockey club. For young children, it usually doesn't matter what team sport they're involved with – just that they're doing something.

With a spread-out family, you may have children at different schools. That always stretches parents. Make friends with other parents so you can car pool. Even if you're too busy to join the Parent/Teacher Association (yours may be called something different), make the effort to talk to other parents at any school function, and encourage play dates.

Case study

A single mother with a long commute to her inner-city law firm used lateral thinking to get away from the worst of the semi-stationary carpark masquerading as the motorway. She moved her children to a different school, this one on the train line. Until then, she had been spending more than two hours each way fighting through heavy traffic.

With the change, even though the children had to leave home a little earlier, her travel was executed much more calmly and efficiently. The family drove 35 minutes to the nearest train station. The two early-teen children disembarked at the station close to their school 25 minutes down the line. Mother then completed the one-hour train ride into the city with no stress, no traffic hassles, no parking and only a short stroll to the office. Although there was not much difference in her travel time, there was a huge difference in her stress levels.

One factor that appeared at first glance to be a disadvantage provided three major benefits. She had to leave work by 4.30 pm in order to catch the train that coordinated with her children's after-school care. Previously she'd regularly worked very long hours.

1. With the new regime she was forced to be more organised with her departure times – this stopped her working silly hours.
2. She could rest and recharge on the train – read, work or nap as she chose.
3. She had daily quality time with the children as they drove to and from the station.

Heather's tip: Allocate buffer time

If at all possible, I add a buffer into my day between having to drop kids at school and having my first meeting. This allows for delays and avoids turning up harried or late.

Heather Douglas.

LESSON 26:

How available should we be for our children?

We've talked about this to some degree in the previous section, specifically in discussion of Maggie Mamen's work. Here is a way to achieve quality time without breaking the 'time bank'.

Personal case study

I'm not suggesting that we have to be 100% available for our children all the time we're in their company. God forbid! That sounds like a very stressful recipe for them as well as their parents. But when we carve out appropriate chunks of time to give them our full attention, we create very special memories for everyone. Even 30 minutes a week makes a difference.

When my six kids were all under 12 we realised that, in the busyness, it was rare to give any one child 'special time' without their siblings interrupting or allowing ourselves to be distracted. So we set up a Special Time system.

Each child had a half hour per week with one parent – the child chose the parent and the activity. We kept track on a fridge chart, with the commitment (appointment) recorded at the beginning of each week.

My only daughter still remembers playing dolls' tea parties with her six-foot farming father. She's now in her early 40s and a busy mother of three, with her own Special Time system.

Special weekends

My niece Jody and her husband have two girls. Here are a couple of 'special time' ideas from her.

'James has an annual "Daddy holiday" with both the girls for a week

by the beach. They have lots of adventures and mischief that would freak me out – and no vegetables! For me, it's the very rare time that I'm at home by myself (a luxury for most mothers).

'Also, every now and then, Dad and one daughter at a time have a sports weekend. Zoe is a Warriors (league) fan and Emma loves the Breakers (basketball). They have the gear, go to games and make it their special time together.'

What can you do, or already do, to deposit wonderful memories in your child's memory bank?

See also:

Lesson 34: *Grandparents and other useful relatives*

LESSON 27:

Make a list of family priorities to help sort the lengthy 'to do' list

In most families there are more things to do than there are hours in the week to do them. These include things like household chores, activities and outings, and friends and relations you want to see more often. It's too easy to get caught up in never-ending deadlines, or on the weekend to sloth around saying: 'I don't feel like it now – I'll get to it some time.'

Changing that emphasis is as simple as making appointments with yourselves – as individuals or as a family.

Start a master list of the big tasks you're putting off until you *'have time'*. Almost always they can be broken down into small chunks and there'll be something you can realistically start on. Other times it does require a solid chunk of time, but hoping spare time will magically show up is never going to happen. We have to plan for it.

Every week, choose one or two activities of long-term and long-lasting value and write them into the family diary or organiser, blocking them in around the commitments of the various family members.

Many families use either a whiteboard or have a family diary on the fridge in order to get a full visual view. Or it could just be a simple wall calendar.

Example

Your three children have sport on Saturdays. You like to go for a long run one day in the weekend and your partner has a regular golf game every Sunday morning. You'd like to visit grandparents this weekend, and the garage is getting messier by the day. For the garage clean-up, the family need to be on hand to sort their personal gear and there never seems to be a gap where everyone can work on it together.

A quick family discussion may mean that some other activities are deferred for the coming weekend in order to find a big enough block of time to get the garage sorted. Equally, it is likely that, apart from the children's sport activities, everything else could be slotted in around the clean-up commitment. However, if we don't take those few minutes to agree on a time-slot, many long-term tasks are constantly deferred because 'we don't have enough time'.

Lisa's tip: Get a family diary

Maintain a family diary in a visible spot. If anyone has a commitment – homework, a costume needed, after school commitments and so on, it must be written in the diary. Try and find something that does a week at a glance.

As soon as you get a school notice, have swimming or music lessons or sports or practices, write it in. On Sunday night, you flip over to the upcoming week and review your commitments. From mother-of-six **Lisa Rose.**

Case study: Weekly planning applied

Some years ago Bryce and Heather were like many farming families – everything needed attention yesterday. They never had enough hours in the day. Although full of good ideas and intentions, they just never got around to putting them into action.

Many people live like this, not enjoying the feeling of being disorganised, but not sure how to change their circumstances. Bryce and Heather did something about it, with the help of a business coach.

Bryce says it's had an immediate impact not only on their farming practices, but also on their personal and family lives and the way they now make choices with their time.

'Every Monday morning Heather and I now have a meeting. We decide what achievements we want for the week. We've got a whiteboard on which we've drawn up the week with a series of timeslots for each day. We then fit the tasks into relevant time slots.

'The key thing that's made a dramatic difference to our lives is blocking in the activities. For instance, we both love to play squash. Now we block it in, and other family activities, as well as the farm jobs. We plan what we **want** to do as well as what we **have** to do.

'This process helps keep us realistic about the time needed, but more than that, it unclutters the mind. Instead of finishing one task and then thinking, 'What shall I do now?' we find we just easily and naturally flow into the next task on the list.

'For instance, I'll come in from the farm after finishing a task, glance at the whiteboard, and instead of wasting time wondering what to do next and often getting distracted into low-level tasks, I just get on with the next scheduled item. The thinking's done once – the focus is then on the action.

'One of the great benefits is that the family has been involved all the way – Heather and I are working together much more, rather than as independent units, and we're also able to do other things we love because our time and our heads have freed up.'

Another consequence, says Bryce, is that Heather has chosen to go back teaching half a day per week. This gives her a fresh interest and stimulation, brings new ideas back into the family and keeps everyone happy.

The family planning system Bryce describes incorporates the same techniques that made a huge difference in my own previously out-of-control life. It's these methods I now share with my clients.

If you'd like a weekly planning sheet to use as a template, incorporating a panel to write in your weekly goals and objectives and integrate them easily into your plan, download my free ebook *How to master time in only 90 seconds* at www.gettingagrip.com

---

Further Help for Planning

If planning and prioritising is a topic you want to master, check out my online course www.gettingagrip.com/product/getting-a-grip-on-planning-and-prioritising-4-part-course/

For readers of this book I have a special discount. When ordering you'll get the chance to apply a code. At the 'Review Order' stage click on 'Redeem Coupon'. Just enter **PARENTING** for an instant $20 discount.

SECTION III
TIME OUT FOR FRAZZLED AND EXHAUSTED PARENTS

LESSON 28:

Create a buffer zone and switch-off time

How about driving home via the scenic route and, if it's a nice day, even taking 10 minutes to walk in the fresh air? That's the occasional strategy of a young working mother of six, including 18-month twins and a blended family with two older children. It helps her transition from work to family before she steps into the welcoming bedlam of home.

Others find that just listening to music, even in heavy traffic or on public transport, creates that buffer or transition zone.

Get rid of the problems of the day as you arrive home

By taking a shower as soon as you walk in and changing clothes, the negative energy is washed away and it changes the mental state.

Case study

A woman working in Victim Support shared with me her favourite switch-off mechanism. Most of us struggle to imagine the kind of tragic and horrible situations she and other community super-heroes, like police, ambulance drivers and firemen, deal with every day.

At her front door is a tall shrub. As she approaches it, she mentally removes the day's problems and tragedies from her mind, depositing them on the shrub, which she has named her 'worry tree'. She can then step inside and be present with her family, leaving work at the door.

In the morning she picks up the burdens and cares again as she steps past the shrub.

Don't turn on the TV

Instead of immediately switching on the TV as you walk in the door, try some quiet relaxing music. Turning on the television is a habit for many, but is it one you want your children to grow up with?

See also:

Lesson 30: *How about a little lie-down*

Lesson 82: *How to still have energy at the end of the day*

LESSON 29:

Create a ten minutes 'quiet zone' and the benefits last an evening!

If you have young children you'll know the routine. You've had a hectic day, you're looking forward to being home with your nearest and dearest, but you know there's a battle zone to contend with before you sit down with your slippers. The little darlings are as keen to see you as you are to be home with them and they've saved up all their day's stories – their trials and tribulations, their joys and successes, to share with Mum and/or Dad.

So, no matter how tired you are, no matter how bad your day's been, you're bombarded with an onslaught of noise as soon as the door opens.

Solution? Teach the children to wait.

Case study

A two-parent family came up with the following creative solution. It could easily be adapted for a single-parent family and any number of different circumstances.

The 10-minute 'quiet zone'

First the explanation to the tribe: *'Daddy is really tired when he gets home; he just needs a few minutes to rest. So, when he gets in, Mum and Dad are going to have a quiet time for 10 minutes. Save your questions, stories and news until we've had our time. Then it's your turn.'*

On the first night of the new regime, with drinks in hand Mum and Dad shut the frosted-glass lounge doors on their dear noise-makers. There were gaps of plain glass amongst the pattern.

For the first couple of nights the parents were amused to see three small noses pressed up against the glass, with giggles and speculation as to just what Mum and Dad were up to. (Nothing too risqué, kids!).

And then the novelty wore off. Within days, it became a non-event. The huge benefit was that this simple strategy calmed everyone down and the evening flowed much more smoothly. Not only did the parents have time to catch their breath but also sibling arguments cut back dramatically. It was so successful that the family continued with the process until the children grew up.

Even if you don't have kids at home, the logic behind the system is great – create separations to help transition from one state to another.

LESSON 30:

How about a little lie-down?

If you're a working parent, think of the last afternoon you sat at your desk, struggling to focus and wishing for matchsticks to prop open your drooping eyelids. You felt guilty. You knew you weren't being productive. *'I must get to bed earlier"* you might have muttered as you dragged yourself off for yet another injection of caffeine.

Or maybe you're a stay-at-home parent. You sat down for a few minutes and suddenly waves of exhaustion, like pounding surf, threatened to topple you. Maybe you've done as I did more than once as a young parent – laid down beside a child to get them to sleep. Perhaps you were reading them a story. Soon after, the child toddled cheerfully out to the lounge while you were sound asleep on the ankle-biter's bed.

Peaks and dips in energy are natural. For most of the day we don't really notice them, but when they hit early-to-midafternoon, if we're carrying a sleep deficit as well, they can lead to the scenarios above.

The problem is that, if we keep artificially pushing through the lows, we put our body into a flight-or-fight response. Do this for long enough and you'll have a health crisis of some kind – either mental or physical. Try running a family when you're sick and you soon realise how important it is to look after yourself.

If you're tired you're inefficient, make mistakes and probably not as patient as you'd like to be.

When you're really tired, could you set aside 10-15 minutes to lie down, meditate, or relax before you start on the next activity? Power napping is an incredibly simple and no-cost productivity tool that brings huge gains.

See also:

Lesson 82: *How to still have energy at the end of the day* (more on power naps)

Lesson 83: *Too tired to think straight? Be a better procrastinator!*

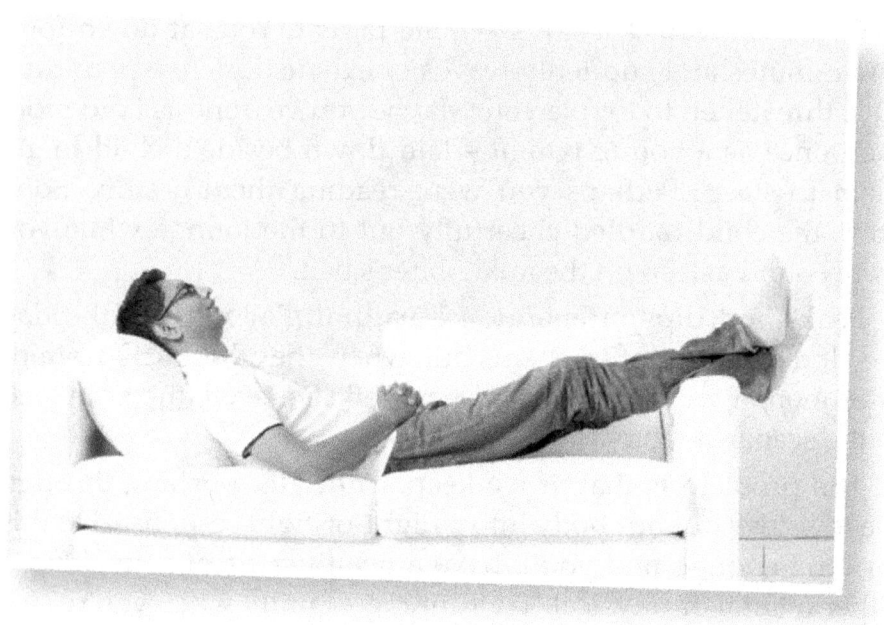

LESSON 31:

Create 'me time' at the start of the day

Get up 30 minutes earlier than the family and use that as your quiet time. The rule in one woman's household was: *'Don't talk to me until I'm ready, and I'll let you know when that is'*. You might use this time for exercise, a wander in the garden, a meditation, prayer or personal study time, or a creative activity you love.

If you don't have small children to organise, it might be longer than 30 minutes.

For many, including myself, it is our most creative time of the day and we'll focus for a couple of hours before coming up for air. When I'm in flow with writing a book, as I am right now, early morning is my most productive time.

One thing NOT to do is look at your email or anything work related. That's a sure recipe for distraction. Your quiet and creative time will disappear down the gurgler so fast you won't even see it vanish.

LESSON 32:

Every six weeks have a 'do nothing' weekend

When you're learning a new job or carrying a very heavy schedule, the temptation is to just keep working into your evenings and weekends.

However, and probably just as well, our bodies were never designed to run non-stop. Think of your body as a rubber band. If it's at stretch all the time it will snap much more quickly than when pressure is released from time to time.

A nutritionist explained it to me this way:

'If you think of all the events in your life as individual stress bricks (positive as well as negative), every time you experience a stressful situation or are particularly busy, you're adding another brick to the stress wall around yourself. If you just keep going, the wall has nowhere to go but up. Many of the people who live this way spend the first part of their annual holidays (if they take them) exhausted and often sick.

'The best way to keep the stress wall at a healthy level – enough to keep you vibrant and alert – is to take a complete break of a few days about every six to eight weeks. This knocks down some of the bricks and keeps the wall always at a manageable height.

'On this weekend, don't take your computer with you, don't take catch-up work, and get someone else to take any work-related calls or emails.'

Case study

Here's how an Australian family incorporated this idea.

When the children were still at home, about every six weeks the family had a do-nothing weekend. Any tasks that *had* to be done were handled on the Thursday night – food shopping, the lawns, essential housework. Then, if they hadn't already decided before, once everyone was home on Friday night, the family had a discussion. The big question they asked themselves was: *'What fun thing(s) shall we do this weekend?'*

Sometimes they quickly packed up, jumped in the car (the kids were big enough to help) and headed out. They might find themselves on the other side of the Blue Mountains, at the beach, somewhere down south (they lived west of Sydney).

Or, they might decide to have an at-home weekend – but no jobs or regular commitments. When they stayed home they often pretended they weren't there. It was a time-out gift to themselves – as if they were on holiday. If they were at home, they all did whatever they wanted. For instance, if someone wanted to stay in bed and read all weekend, that was a fine choice – because it was their choice.

The lady sharing this story finished by saying: *'It is such a powerful strategy and we get such great benefits from it that my husband and I still hold to the same system, even though the chicks have flown the nest.'*

Another case study

A young mother on one of my sessions had a variation on the tip above. Her family didn't have much disposable income so leaving home regularly wasn't in the budget.

'We tell our friends and family that we're going away for the weekend. We shut the gate, pull the curtains in the front rooms, and leave the answerphone on.

'But we stay home. The kids romp around in the back yard, sometimes we just run around in our pyjamas all day, and we have a wonderful rest. It's as good as a holiday.'

What delightful 'treats' can you institute in your home? We all need time to recharge. Life shouldn't be all hard work and rush, rush, rush.

If you'd like an attractive reminder list of 'take time for me' ideas, just download *23 Simple Strategies to Keep You Sane, Happy & Healthy* from gettingagrip.com/simplestrategies.

LESSON 33:

What I learnt about stress management from a pack of kids

I'd taken a day off to go beachcombing with four of my grandchildren, who ranged in age from three to eight at the time. Three things combined to create a weekday that felt like a delicious holiday, despite the pile of work waiting:

- It was school holidays
- It was wedding anniversary time-out for their hard-working parents
- I'd made a conscious decision to be like the kids and to just take the day as it came.

At the end of a perfect day, four tired and happy babes were returned to their loving parents, somewhat grubby from mud-larking in the estuary. Their totally relaxed and content grandmother sat down with a glass of red wine to write her regular Top Time Tips newsletter.

As I began to write, the most amazing sunset became the backdrop to the computer screen. Small evening sounds filled the quiet air. Seabirds chirped as they fluffed their feathers for the night, the last of a flock of Mallard ducks waddled back to their nests, and a fisherman zipped up the channel, heading home for dinner. It really was the perfect end to a perfect day, and I realised that the wonderful feeling of peace and contentment was more intense than normal. Years later, I can still remember that sensation of calm.

Whenever I notice something a little different I like to dig a bit deeper. Three lessons were reinforced as I reflected on the day.

Live in the moment

How easy it is to be amazingly reinvigorated by the small pleasures of life when we can live in the moment, as children do. No matter where we work, but possibly even more when it's from home, it's incredibly easy to get sucked into the pressure of work, forget to stop, forget to notice the little details, the serendipitous moments and events. I'd made a deliberate decision that morning to just 'be' with the kids; the rewards were far beyond my expectations.

Have you ever noticed that if you try and combine 'play' and 'work' your mind is too cluttered and you miss too much? And how many times do we wish we had more time with loved ones and then try to do other things at the same time? I know I've certainly been guilty of that many times.

It's not about the money

I don't know about you, but in times past I've caught myself thinking that I had to get away on expensive holidays in order to have a break. But this beach day cost nothing and we had as much fun as anything I'd done in ages, even including a wonderful trip to Singapore a few weeks earlier.

Chunk your activities

I'd invoked a very useful time-management principle – one that helps us in our work as well as our play: the power of 'chunking' or concentrated focus. If we chunk our activities so that we're fully present and engaged in one activity for a set period of time, we achieve far more than if we try to keep multiple activity balls in the air simultaneously.

On this particular day it seemed that an inverse ratio kicked in – a greater than normal degree of focused concentration returned a far higher than normal level of satisfaction and a sense of accomplishment for time well spent.

Here's to achieving your targets without working yourself to death – by using time like a little child.

Two other tips on focus

Andrea's tip: Squawking toddler? Focus!

Your toddler is asking for attention by clinging to you? Straight away give him or her five – ten minutes of full attention. (You won't need more). It works a treat. You'll then be able to walk away and focus on your own tasks while they carry on with their play.

Kate's tip: A fast start gets amazing results

Break the back of a big task with a fast focus and concentrated action. Tell yourself you're just making a start. You'll be amazed – you'll achieve 80% of the results in 20% of the time.

Put on a favourite CD and go as hard as you can for one song. This works wonders with kids, especially if you let them choose the song. You will be astounded at what you can achieve in three or four minutes, particularly if you have three or four pairs of hands working together.
Kate Booker

LESSON 34:

Grandparents and other useful relatives

(Sometimes grandparents are the principal caregiver – this snippet is provided for those who don't have their little ones living with them.)

It's tough being a parent; you need all the help and support you can get. Concerned ring-siders can be very helpful. They're not worn down by the day-to-day minutiae and often bring a fresh but mature perspective. Just a few minutes' conversation can bring a whole new way of looking at things. If you're lucky enough to have willing family nearby, make the most of this.

Surprisingly often I've heard older people say wistfully, *'I'd love to have my grandchild to stay, but my family seems reluctant to share.'*

Obviously if a relative is not a trustworthy person nothing further needs to be said. But let's focus on the norm, not the few dangerous and dysfunctional people who seem to hog the news. There are several possible scenarios here.

It could be that a young parent is clingy and overprotective. As a result they put stress on their health and marriage because they never get a child-free break. They also selfishly deny children and grandparents the chance to have a meaningful relationship. But there's the other side of the story too. Some grandparents, usually grandmothers, are hyper-critical. That doesn't help either!

Of course, not every grandparent wants to be, or is able to be, involved. They may be working full-time, or live too far away, or there are age or health reasons. I count my blessings that I had my children young enough that I still have enough energy and resilience to enjoy being their backup resource when they want help.

Fortunately I'm my own boss. I just book myself out on the dates the family need me. However, because there are so many of them and I've got a very active business and social life, my families, including my nearby niece, know they have to book in early to get me. And I have been known to say 'no' if it doesn't work for me – without guilt!

Rules of engagement for the grandparent-type person

Be prepared to share, be prepared to help, but try not to interfere or comment unless you're invited. It's not always easy and I know I've sometimes over-stepped the mark, but for the sake of harmony in the family it's worth making an effort.

However, when you're the adult in charge, be prepared to discipline appropriately. Years ago a situation came up with one of the older grandchildren. I took him out to the garage away from the other siblings and gave him a verbal dressing down. It wasn't our normal kind of interaction so it had a strong impact; he took it on the chin and didn't argue back, as he might have done with his parents.

When I reported the incident to his mother on her return she was very appreciative. She had been worried about this particular behaviour in her son.

If you haven't got convenient grandparents, are there other relatives who can help? Aunties, uncles, cousins … or older neighbours with the interest and capacity.

Case studies

Helping with the manners

When her grandchildren were young Sue used to put on the occasional 'posh dinner' with lovely table settings, elegant plates and a range of cutlery. She had two motivations: to teach them good manners, and also to create a memorable experience with them. However, it had a further unexpected consequence. A visitor noticed their excellent table manners and as a result, two of the children were invited to participate as audience on a TV cooking show.

(As a slightly off-topic aside, my youngest son Maurice experienced the opposite of this when involved with running an Army programme for young unemployed persons. Phil, aged 17, did not know how to use a knife and fork. His family had only ever eaten takeaways in front of TV. By the time the Army had finished with him his social skills had been significantly expanded and he blossomed into a much more confident young man.)

The big camp out weekend

One grandfather has an annual camp-out weekend for all his grandchildren over the age of 10. It has become THE event that all the kids look forward to each year, and the younger ones aspire to.

The shopping trip weekend

Another quite wealthy family takes each grandchild on a weekend trip from New Zealand to Sydney when they reach 16.

Each of these examples is a special occasion. They don't have to cost a lot of money. The key is that the children and their grandparents are creating memories and shared experiences.

LESSON 35:

Find a supply of good babysitters

Start or join a Babysitting Club – it's free!

This was a god-send for me when the children were young. At the time we were living miles away from any family and certainly didn't have money for babysitters.

While there will be more modern tech-based methods now, in my day this is how it worked:

- Friends invited friends until we had a group of about 15 – 20 families. We didn't all know each other initially but everyone was considered trustworthy.
- We kept a record of all names and details and everyone had a list of the other members' contact details.
- Each family managed the 'babysitting book' for a month and was responsible for finding a sitter when required.
- No money changed hands. When you did a job you were credited hours. When you used the service you were debited hours.
- It wasn't just mothers who babysat; sometimes a father was the nominated sitter.
- Usually the children were fed and mostly in bed before the sitter arrived (depending on their age and the time of day.)
- Occasionally you'd have someone's kids for a day or a weekend.

Less formal methods

Encourage your children to bring friends home for play dates, so you can get to know their families and also build up credits. Then you can take turns when help is needed.

It often works best, if you've got two or more children, for them to go to different friends' homes if you're going to be away for more than a few hours. They're with their own buddies and it's not too much of a burden for the other family.

Hiring a babysitter

Teenagers and students are a great source, but also consider single parents trying to earn a few extra dollars, especially if they can bring their own child.

If your children are old enough, quiz them the next day to find out whether the sitter engaged with them or just let them run riot.

Tips for a great relationship with your babysitter

- Pay fairly, pay cash, have the correct change and don't ask for credit.
- Tell them what they need to know. Include a checklist: bedtimes, medications, and emergency numbers.
- Explain what you expect of them e.g. assume teenage babysitters will be on the phone from the moment your children are in bed (and sometimes earlier!) to the moment your car pulls up. If you'd prefer they weren't, make this clear ahead of time.
- Give them as much notice as possible of a cancellation and consider paying a nominal 'cancellation fee' if it's within 48 hours (one or two hours' wage, depending on what you normally pay).
- Be back at the time you say you will. Phone if you've been delayed and don't make a habit of it.
- Create a list of 10 or so reliable babysitters so you have others to fall back on if your regular person is unavailable.
- Ask friends with kids of the same age for recommendations.

- When one good babysitter is unavailable, ask if they have a reliable friend they'd recommend.

Optimise the time they're in the house

You're paying for their time anyway. Consider paying a little more if your sitter is prepared to do some small household jobs such as ironing, washing up or making school lunches once the kids are in bed.

SECTION IV:
TIPS AND TECHNIQUES FOR DAILY EFFICIENCIES

LESSON 36:

Teach everyone to become a 'walking question mark'

There are always better ways to do things. Every time you do a task, look for ways to trim a few seconds or a minute off. They mount up to a surprising total over a week. Time-saving efficiencies are all around us but most people don't go looking for them. Instead, they just complain about lack of time!

Two simple examples:

- Stop a child from running around carrying one thing when they could save steps by carrying three or four items at the same time. Teach the children to ask themselves: *'How can I do this task more efficiently and quickly?'*
- To quickly put away the cutlery, lay a tea towel on the bench right beside the cutlery drawer. Tip the contents of the cutlery basket onto the tea towel, then you can efficiently pick up and put away each category. (It's a bit like a kitchen version of the childhood game Pick-up-Sticks.)

The following excerpt from *Getting a Grip on the Paper War,* one of my earlier books, expands on this theme. Even if you've read it, I think you'll enjoy a repeat of the story.

> *The field of time and motion study movement was first recognised as a science back in 1910. Industrial engineers Frank Gilbreth and his wife Lillian were among the first in the scientific management field. They were also two of the earliest to develop the science of motion study and quickly earned the title of efficiency experts.*

Although their achievements were very relevant and useful in the business world of the day, two of their twelve children took their accomplishments to a far wider audience. If you can find a copy of Cheaper By The Dozen by Frank B Gilbreth Jr and Ernestine Gilbreth Carey your efforts will be rewarded. It's a very humorous look at how Father Frank tried his theories on his family. And no, I won't loan my tatty old copy – it's precious! (There is a movie with the same name, based on the Gilbreth family, but not as good as the book.)

Here are a couple of snippets:

'Dad took moving pictures of us children washing dishes, so that he could figure out how we could reduce our motions and thus hurry through the task. Irregular jobs, such as painting the back porch or removing a stump from the front lawn, were awarded on a low-bid basis. Each child who wanted extra pocket money submitted a sealed bid saying what he would do the job for. The lowest bidder got the contract.

'At home or on the job, Dad was always the efficiency expert. He buttoned his vest from the bottom up, instead of from the top down, because the bottom-to-top process took him only three seconds, while the top-to-bottom took seven. He even used two shaving brushes to lather his face, because he found that by so doing he could cut seventeen seconds off his shaving time. For a while he tried shaving with two razors, but he finally gave that up.

"I can save forty-four seconds," he grumbled, "but I wasted two minutes this morning putting this bandage on my throat." It wasn't the slashed throat that really bothered him. It was the two minutes.'

You think such a philosophy is restrictive? In fact it creates freedom by freeing up valuable time from mundane and repetitive tasks, whilst still achieving the necessary result.

From Getting a Grip on the Paper War by Robyn Pearce

LESSON 37:

Share the chores

Many families make a household duty roster and place it on the fridge door. Include cooking, bathroom tidy-up, trash, pets and dishes. Even three- and four-year-olds can make a contribution – and you're teaching them life-long habits. It's also a great way to save arguments about whose turn it is.

Meal preparation can be shared

A five-year-old can set the table, wash vegetables and rip up lettuce for a salad. Kids as young as seven or eight can prepare a simple meal with minimal supervision. Tinned soup and cheese on toast tastes pretty good if you're tired and you don't have to cook it yourself.

Children actually take pride in having responsibility for such a 'grown up' thing as dinner. It not only shares the load, but shares the kudos when dinner is delicious!

Consider nominating each family member to cook at least one meal every week. They don't have to produce a gastronomic treat. Adopt the rule *'if it's on the table and it's edible – it's dinner!'*

Instead of a roster, some families work as a team after dinner, except the cook, in clearing the table, loading the dishwasher, dropping tablecloth or place mats (if you use cloth ones) into the washing hamper and wiping over the table. When you work as a team, the dining room and kitchen can be clean and tidy in less than 10 minutes.

Heather's tip: Triage the day's crop of tasks and delegate where possible

I triage unexpected problems and daily tasks into those that can be knocked off quickly but are not so important, those that are important but need time and concentration, and those that need to be delegated (to family, friends or some other resource) or ditched because they are time consuming but not important to our immediate needs. **Heather Douglas**

LESSON 38:

Hire a student for the hell hour

My fifth child was a baby and I was at the doctor's. That was a fairly regular occurrence; the whole gang arrived in exactly nine years (to the day!). After he'd finished with Jimmy's examination, Dr Forbes, himself a father of six, turned his attention to me.

'You're looking a bit peaky,' he commented.

'I never seem to get enough sleep, and there's always just too much to do,' I replied with a sigh.

And then he dished out some of the best advice I ever had as a young mother: *'Hire a schoolgirl for the Hell Hour.'*

We were a one-income family and a very small income at that. Money was scarce and the only way I could make ends meet was to take in boarders. However, his advice was appealing so I counted my pennies and rearranged the priorities. A couple of enquiries uncovered Leonie, a helpful 14-year-old from just along the road.

For the next six months, while the current baby was small and I was in that particularly overwhelmed state, Leonie hopped off the school bus every afternoon at our place instead of hers. She would grab a sandwich for afternoon tea and then work solidly for an hour – for about the hourly rate she would have earned working at McDonald's. Once things eased a bit, she reduced to a couple of times a week for another year and then returned to five nights a week when the last baby arrived.

It was fantastic. She did anything I needed: bringing in the washing; bathing the bigger kids; peeling potatoes; picking up toys; even the ironing. And so I had my first big lesson in leverage and delegation. An extra pair of hands was the life-saver

I needed. Many parents, and especially mothers, frequently feel really frazzled – there is so much to do that it seems you never catch up and, more importantly, you often feel as though you're short-changing your little ones on quality time.

It's also great for the contributory dads who aim to get home early enough to be involved with their small children's bedtime. Some of the routine tasks will have been handled and they're more likely to arrive home to a calmer house and a less exhausted wife.

And there's another factor in today's families that few women of my generation had to worry about. Many modern women hold down a full-time job outside the home or, as in the case of two of my families, the wives are working in their family businesses, a building company and a farm. Somehow that all squeezes in around the domestics, child-rearing and a raft of other activities.

If you're feeling overwhelmed, stop for a moment and consider the following:

- Could you use the help of a student?
- A cleaner for two to three hours a week/fortnight will get all the basics done faster than you, because they're focused on one thing.
- Have you ever thought of sending out the ironing? See if you can find a local ironing service that picks up and drops off from your house. (Or buy wrinkle-free linen and garments.)
- If you can't afford help on a weekly or fortnightly basis, consider hiring a home or garden 'spring cleaner' as needed for big jobs like cleaning the windows and oven, chopping back trees or unclogging the gutters.
- What about a reliable student to run bigger kids to after-school activities?
- Lawns aren't your thing? High school kids are always looking for cash.

Maybe you feel like you can't afford it. Consider this:

- How would it feel to come home to a clean tidy house?
- How would your family's quality of life improve if you had less chores to do? What else could you do with that free time?
- You may even save money in other areas. For example, Louise found hiring a cleaner for three hours a week meant that she had more time to cook and spent less on take-away food.

There are always variations on this theme, of course. As you've already read, I'm a great advocate of making older kids responsible for their share of the chores so they learn to be responsible adults. Maybe some of their pocket money is linked to satisfactory performance of certain home tasks. But when they're little and you're trying to do everything, get help. It's not being weak – it's being realistic.

We don't need to do everything. Super-parents are often exhausted and burnt-out. We're in this for a long time, not a perfect time.

You'll find an alternative way of engaging small helpers at **Lesson 66:** *A creative way for technology to be your friend*

LESSON 39:

Wish you had another pair of hands for some of your work?

If you're running a small or home-based business and a family, the following experience may be helpful. It's related to the previous lesson but from a slightly different angle.

In a business context we're well aware of the importance of delegation as a powerful time-saving technique. As parents we're also very aware of the need to teach our children good work habits. The two can blend. Experience from one arena can transfer to the other. Children can learn life lessons disguised as business opportunities and we can get help.

Some years ago two school mums worked part-time for me. Kate was my marketing assistant and one of her tasks included helping to produce my bi-monthly newsletter – the hard copy forerunner of my Top Time Tips ezine (which these days goes to over 12,000 people around the world with the click of a few keystrokes).

Kate's help was a godsend. The recipient list was constantly growing and processing the newsletter was quite a chore. I wrote the content and then she took over. She formatted it, took the original to the copy shop to run off, folded the 600-plus newsletters, ran the labels out of our database, stuck them on envelopes, stuffed and stamped the envelopes, and then delivered the finished product to the post office. It was quite a time-consuming job.

One day she arrived at work bubbling with enthusiasm. She explained that she'd come up with a better way for the job to be done, saving me money and us both time. Dylan, her 12-year old son, would like to tender for the more manual component of the job at a lower hourly rate than I paid Kate.

That seemed like a good idea so we set the wheels in motion, for the next newsletter was due. A few days later Kate came in waving a piece of paper – Dylan's invoice.

'*That's great,*' I said, looking at a very minimal amount of money (in comparison with what she would have earned for the same work). '*What a brilliant example of outsourcing!*'

'*Oh, it gets better than that,*' Kate replied. '*Dylan decided he could outsource too. He got his 6-year-old brother doing the stamps and a mate who could do the same work as him to the same standard; their pay was a meal at McDonald's!*'

I wonder what Dylan is doing now. Something entrepreneurial, I wouldn't be surprised!

How can you adapt Dylan's example?

If you've got work that could be outsourced, you might not have children of an appropriate age to help. We've already talked about teenage students as one source, but who else can take some of your load?

Where to find assistance

- Use school newsletters to seek helpers.
- Put an ad in your local community paper.
- Are there students in your area needing work experience for a few hours a week?
- What about a student job scheme? Most colleges and universities run these. I found a fantastic young architectural student for a short-term collating and typing job – she had a brilliant brain, was a fast typist, incredibly accurate and a pleasure to have in the office. She was seriously over-qualified for the job but she wanted money and didn't mind how basic the work was. She ploughed through my project in half the time I would have taken, in part because she could focus on that one task.

- Try an ad on the notice board at the local pre-school, childcare centre or kindergarten. Mums make great workers, as long as you can be flexible with sick children and school holidays.
- Can someone work offsite for you? For about 11 years I had a wonderful office manager who initially worked in my office but continued to do so after the family moved over 1000 kilometres away. We saw each other once in a blue moon but talked regularly and emailed all the time. Mail and couriers did the rest. It worked brilliantly, not just for us, but also for her children who were still at school. She was able to deal with all their needs – and hold down a job she liked instead of having to resign because they'd shifted towns.
- Grandparents, semi-retired people, immigrants, solo parents desperate for a bit of extra cash – all are fantastic and appreciative resources.

If it's an older person, you're helping your community as much as they're contributing to your family. If it's a young person you've employed, you're teaching them valuable life lessons at the same time. Seems like a win-win to me!

LESSON 40:

What my grandsons taught me about multi-tasking

Ever felt overwhelmed with too much stuff in your space and a spinning head?

I think I'm pretty good at clearing clutter and keeping focused but one day I fell back into the insidious bog of overwhelm – and two of my grandbabies bookmarked the lesson.

The one-year-old had just been weaned so, to my delight, Mum and Dad seized the chance to have a child-free weekend.

The two days were as busy as you'd expect with two little boys. Cars, soft toys, wooden blocks and dinosaurs littered my normally immaculate house. Two-year-old Joel practised his loudest and fastest driving skills on the beaten-up old plastic bike I'd kept tucked away for small visitors. Baby Luke's smiling face kept popping up in unexpected places as he practised his crawling skills.

Between multiple rounds of sleeping, eating and cleaning up, we fitted in walks, a harbour cruise on the local tourist excursion boat and a visitor who brought her own toy box of new and tantalisingly different treasures.

However, there was one small challenge. Amongst the joys of playing Granny, I had to fit in a few hours of my own work. Normally I avoid grown-up work when I've got kids to play with but a very important deadline had queue-jumped.

The baby had his usual sleep time, the toddler was easily seduced by Winnie the Pooh on DVD, and I made some progress for an hour.

Then, picture this scene:

It's Sunday afternoon. Awake again, the baby was bopping,

the toddler was doing Tigger bounces (sometimes on top of his brother – why did I let him watch Winnie the Pooh?) and the floor was even more littered with toys. The children's dinner was under way and their parents were a couple of hours away. Important papers were tangoing with the tomatoes, and my laptop was humming on the kitchen bench. (Anywhere else and someone might have killed either themselves or the computer.)

My brain was starting to fry and I was feeling stressed and uncomfortable. Why? What was wrong? Suddenly it hit me.

'What am I doing?' I exclaimed to the baby.

With a sense of purpose missing from the previous few hours I zoomed in, switched off the distracting lump of metal on the bench and put everything remotely looking like big person work where it belonged: in my office down the hall.

Back in the kitchen I looked around. The child chaos was just the same but a huge ton of stress had vanished. And then I realised – the sense of freedom was exactly the same as my clients describe when I've taught them how to clean up their offices.

This simple domestic scene had at least three messages:

- Every item in our space is connected to us with an invisible energy cord. If you ask yourself, *'Does this energise me, or weigh me down?'* you'll quickly know if you should shift or eliminate something.
- The heavy feeling was because I was trying to do incompatible activities. Multi-tasking has its place, but this wasn't one of them. The result was dissatisfaction and stress. I wasn't giving my best to my two dear little grandsons; nor could I concentrate enough to produce quality work.
- We all need reminders. I know this stuff, and I still got seduced by trying to do two things at the same time.

In case you're wondering, I easily completed the proposal once the family had left and I could concentrate.

If you're the parent and can't hand the wee darlings back, chunk your time. Don't try and do complex work while attending to small-people needs. Dodging from task to task is inefficient and a sure recipe for frustration.

Andrea's tip: Don't try to squeeze everything in

Make yourself a day-plan, schedule your tasks and stick to that list as closely as possible. If anything extra interrupts your plan, don't try to squeeze everything in! Think about the plan (list) and simply cross out, postpone or cancel the least important task.

See also:

Lesson 78: *How good are you at multi-tasking?*

LESSON 41:

What I learnt from the messy toy box

My grandchildren are great teachers. Three time-management principles were reinforced for me some years ago when I looked after a nearly walking one-year-old Matt and his three-year-old brother, Corin, for a week.

1. Complete actions the first time

This applies even to something as simple as getting dressed. On the first day I wandered downstairs in my dressing gown, thinking I'd have a shower later. Bad idea – I should have dressed as soon as I got out of bed. Once the baby was up, the quiet moments to attend to ablutions vanished until he went down for his mid-morning nap. Luckily no one knocked on the door or they'd have found me still in my nightie.

In your world, how often do multiple interruptions bounce at you? For most of us, parents or not, it happens frequently. So how do you handle the interruptions? Do you control them, or do they control you? If we're not careful, we end up with projects and incomplete tasks layered all over every spare inch of workspace.

Instead, take that extra moment or two to complete things or, at very least take them to a natural stopping point before letting the next highly important matter railroad your good intentions.

2. Get ready first

On the second day I had a hair appointment. With two little ones, you can't just down tools and dash out the door (my normal style when going a couple of minutes down the road to my hairdresser). Instead, preparation involved gathering raisins, bananas, water, nappies and shoes, putting car seats in the car, taking the toddler to the toilet, getting a flannel for sticky fingers, plus extra time to get them in and out of the car ... Not knowing how long it would take, I got ready well ahead of time. We turned up at the hair salon so early even the hairdresser was surprised!

The same concept applies in all of life. If you find yourself often running late for appointments, stressed, flustered or behind the mark in some way, perhaps you're not preparing early enough.

Instead, at the beginning of the day or even the day before, do a mental check list of the coming day's activities. Lay everything out long before you need it and then carry on with other tasks until it's time to change activity. It's such a simple thing – yet it takes away a huge amount of pressure.

3. Cut the clutter – 'minimalism' is good!

On the third morning I had a long-standing speaking engagement, booked months before I was asked to babysit. Time to call in the favours. Daughter Catherine and her slightly older pre-school sons came over to help look after the little cousins. By the time I returned home that afternoon four small boys had pulled almost everything out of the large toy cupboard. Wooden blocks, cars, soft toys, balls of all shapes, puzzles, Lego, playing cards, books... you name it, it was there – carpeting the floor.

Cath offered to clean up before heading home.

'Don't worry about the mess, dear,' I said. *'The two little ones will only pull things out again as soon as you've gone. I'll pick up tonight when they're in bed.'*

That night I was tired so I decided to leave things where they lay. The next morning Corin and Matt poked at the heap of toys but nothing much seemed to hold their attention for long.

By the afternoon of day four I couldn't stand the clutter any longer. With baby Matt tucked up for his afternoon nap I swung into action, assisted by Corin. As you'd expect, there was great satisfaction in finding my carpet again. Clean space really works for me! However, the real 'aha' was in the behaviour of the boys. While the floor was littered with 'stuff' they seemed quite scattered and irritable. As soon as the house was tidy and they only had a few toy items to choose from, they calmed right down. And, whatever they then chose to play with got lengthy focus instead of the previous *'look and discard'* treatment I'd observed when there was so much choice.

Whether you're a senior executive with a huge workload or a busy parent with a houseful of small children:

- Keep things pared down to basics.
- Put away what's not being used right now.
- Only get things out when you really need them.

No matter what the age, clutter equals confusion, lack of focus and irritability.

Wisdom from other parents on minimising mess

To speed up the tidying, place a basket in the room you're cleaning and into it put anything that doesn't go in that room. Empty the basket once at the end. It's FAST. **Collette.**

Forget big toy boxes. Have a bunch of smaller boxes. Get one out at a time. There's less to pick up and the kids appreciate getting a 'fresh' bunch of toys when you choose a different box. **Karen.**

My tip on toy boxes

A slight variation on Karen's tip about toy boxes: when my own six were little, despite our limited means, the kids still had a lot of toys, thanks to kind grandparents and other family members.

However, the volume of toys created a big nightly tidy-up job – until we hit on a solution. We put half of them away in storage and every few months swapped them over. The children loved being reunited with their half-forgotten favourites, the toy clutter was halved, and we saved time every day with less to put away.

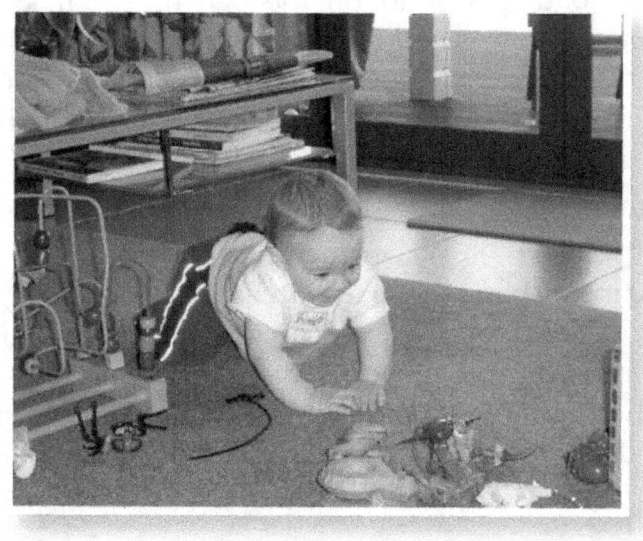

LESSON 42:

Have a special place for the school gear

Get the bags off the floor

It's common for children to leave their bags lying around underfoot. If they do empty them, they often leave vital documents floating around on the bench. You'll know from experience that notices and homework risk disappearing under magazines, newspapers and sofa cushions, being used as paper darts by the youngest candidate for the air force, or chewed by the dog.

How about a basket on the bench for all school-related paperwork?

Can you install bag pegs in the kitchen, hall or laundry? Young children are used to bag pegs at school so it shouldn't be hard to get compliance from the troops. Instruct the bag owners to get their lunch boxes, school notices and homework out, and then hang their bags up as soon as they walk in the door from school.

The benefits

- You don't spend the evening tripping over school bags.
- Anything for school (homework, notes for teachers, reading books…) can be placed straight into their bags.
- In the morning, you and the children have one less thing to worry about.
- Crawling or toddling members of the rug-rat brigade are less likely to riffle through their older siblings' bags if they're out of reach.

Diane's tips on organisation

- *Give each child a cloth bag that hangs from the edge of the table or over the door. They can put finished things in there each day. They then only have one place to look for books, homework or anything else they need for school or extra-curricula activities.*

- *If you have space in your entry way, have a box for each child to hold their backpack and school stuff. You can put things you find in the house in it as well.*

- *When they're at the age of bringing home lots of paintings, worksheets and art work, post a contribution once a month to grandparents, godparents, and other relations. Also, let the child choose one picture per month to keep in a Clearfile. You'll have a nice record without too much clutter.* **Diane Lithgow.**

LESSON 43:

*Sh*t will happen – plan for it!*

If you work in the corporate world, you might have experienced this; you've got a briefcase under one arm, the baby under the other, and you're walking out the door. You're mentally rehearsing your presentation for an 8:30 meeting which you will just make if you really put your foot down after stopping at the crèche when … the baby spits up on your tie or new blouse.

Bruce reports: *' I mentally beat myself up every time this type of thing happens and yet I know there was nothing I could have done to prevent it – it's just part of life when you have young children.'*

What can you do to anticipate the emergencies?

- Brand new pantyhose *will* ladder.
- Babies *will* spill sour milk on your best suit.
- The drain *will* mysteriously overflow when you're already running late.

Rather than reacting to these situations when they arrive, adopt a proactive approach. What possible solutions might save your blood pressure?

For example

- Keep an ironed shirt and a clean tie in the office. If you use it, replace it.
- Make sure you have a new pair of pantyhose (or two!) and a couple of tampons in your desk drawer.
- Keep an old purse with $50 in it in a safe place in case of emergency.

- Have a list of emergency numbers on your mobile: babysitters, plumber, electrician, doctor, dentist, garage, breakdown service.
- Consider sourcing a personal concierge service so you're ready for unexpected crises.
- Always carry a hairbrush, wet flannel and a pack of wet wipes when you're transporting kids. They can polish each other up as you negotiate traffic. (I don't recommend using wet wipes on faces. Many are coated with chemicals. In fact, I don't like thinking about what they do to a baby's skin, but we won't go there for now.)

When the wheels do fall off and you get taken by surprise, take a few minutes as soon as the crisis is dealt with to set up emergency procedures for the next time.

You might not anticipate everything but at least you'll be better prepared for some things.

LESSON 44:

Four simple strategies to save the morning madness

1. Have shoes ready the night before

Find and clean the shoes and put them by the door, ready to be slipped on as the troops dash by. (Unless you've got a chewy puppy, in which case they can go on top of the washing machine, or some other item reachable by children, but inaccessible for all but a St Bernard.)

2. Don't sleep in!

Tempting as it is after a late night, or an extra glass of wine with a mate, the payback is too horrible.

Think back to the days before sleepless nights and nose-wrinkling nappies. Even then, a late start on a working day got you off on the wrong foot. Now you've got more feet to get wrong. Murphy's Law will always prevail – as soon as you start to get uptight, the little poppets will go on strike.

Don't short-change yourself with too little time. Setting your alarm too late or hitting the snooze button one too many times will put you in panic mode and on the run from the moment you get up, setting a rushed tone to your whole day. And the children will react – everything that can go wrong will, and it's not their fault (much as you'd like a handy scapegoat). You'll have set up a stress cycle from the moment you stepped late out of bed.

Instead, work out how long you and the kids need to be out the door at a comfortable time and then allow a further 15 minutes. Have the discipline to get up when the alarm goes off.

3. Be realistic

Don't try to achieve too much in the mornings. Unless you're an early-morning person who thrives on 5am starts, your morning milestones should be as simple as this:

- Wake up.
- Shower and dress.
- Get the kids dressed.
- Get everyone fed and out the door.
- Leave the house tidy(ish) behind you.

4. Get ready first

Get yourself ready first before attending to the children. Teach them the same habit. When they're ready, they can read, play, or do an approved activity they enjoy.

LESSON 45:

Use lists

Some families use lists to help keep children focused on their morning tasks.

Suggestion: don't put more than five things on the list. This saves the young brains from being overloaded with too much data, plus it's easier for rushing parents to oversee.

Be specific and stick to the important stuff. For example:

Getting up

- Make bed.
- Pyjamas under pillow.
- Dirty clothes in laundry basket.
- All clothes and toys off the floor.
- Towels hung up.

Getting out the door

- Have breakfast.
- Clean teeth.
- Brush hair.
- Lunch and books in school bag.
- Feed guinea pig.

Some related tips

- If you have a pre-reader use pictures or symbols as well as words.

- Lucy Ryan's tip: Have a 'To Do' list and a 'Done' list side by side. As the prompt, use photos of the child doing the tasks. With Velcro on the back of the photos, the child has the satisfaction of shifting the photo from one list to the other when the task is finished.
- Make it colourful and easy to read.
- Put the list where everyone can see it.
- Have a column to tick off when done. We all like that sense of completion and satisfaction.
- An agreed number of ticks might generate a reward of some kind, preferably something other than time on screens (See also: **Lesson 67:** *How is screen time impacting your children?*)
- Lists take the pressure off you to keep tracking where the children are up to. They work particularly well with boys and children with ADHD. These kids need a great deal of help to stay on track and simple lists are a great aid.
- Give the big ones responsibility for the little ones.

LESSON 46:

Turn departure time into a game, with you as mission control

Wherever possible, give kids responsibility for getting themselves ready. Any school-aged child can dress themselves, make toast or pour milk over cereal, wash their face and brush their hair and teeth. See your role as Project Manager – you oversee, check everything has been done and trouble-shoot, but leave 'operational' issues to the troops themselves.

Karen and her family developed a fun game. It started as a bit of a joke but turned into a very useful tool. She called herself 'Mission Control' and her three children 'Red 1', 'Red 2' and 'Red 3'.

Morning conversations went something like this:

'Mission Control to Red 2 – do you copy, Red 2?'

'Red 2 to Mission Control – I read you loud and clear.'

'Red 2, please report on status of breakfast.'

'I had toast and peanut butter.'

'Thank you, Red 2, and what is the status of your shoes and socks?'

'Umm ... just about to put them on, Mission Control.'

'Thank you, Red 2. Report when done. Over and out.'

LESSON 47:

Minimise makeup routines

Find ways to apply the 80/20 rule, which in the context of time can be interpreted to say that 80% of your results will be achieved by 20% of the effort.

For example, Tina says: *'I can get in and out of the bathroom in less than half an hour. I found that if I don't blow-dry my hair it looks terrible but if I blow-dry just the front and sides, the back seems to fall into line. This takes half the time I used to spend.*

Also, I used to wash my hair every day but I've found I can easily get away with every second day. In fact, it's easier to style on a day I haven't washed it.'

Develop a quick-fix hairstyle you can do in two minutes flat and that looks neat and professional even if you're having a bad hair day. Most medium to long styles look good brushed sleek and flat and held by an attractive clip at the nape of the neck. An Alice band can also be a lifesaver.

Consider paring your make-up routine back. For example, you might find you look almost as good by applying only lipstick and mascara, skipping foundation, concealer and eye make-up.

And have you thought about dyeing your lashes and brows. A colour job will typically last six to eight weeks.

LESSON 48:

Make the bed as soon as you get out of it

Penny was a participant in a group of English CEOs I was working with in London. Her dad was a 2 Star General and she learnt some great life-long attitudes and habits from him.

'Every morning I would wake up to him knocking on my door saying: "Time to get up. Another day in which to excel."

'One of his other favourite maxims was: "Make the bed as soon as you get out of it." His rationale was that no matter how your day goes, you have accomplished one thing. Even if you have a bad day you return to a well-made bed.'

As Penny shared her Dad's wisdom on that hot London day, I had a flashback to a younger Robyn. In my earlier adult years I was a very sloppy housekeeper. It was my lovely mother-in-law, Molly, who triggered my transformation.

Her house-keeping methods were far superior to mine. She never criticised my untidiness but I began to notice the sense of calm when I walked into her house, even if my six young children were running in behind (or ahead of) me. Her home was always tidy, well-maintained and attractive. Bit by bit, using her as an aspirational model, my methods improved. One of those practices was to make the bed before leaving the bedroom.

As well as setting the tone for the whole day, if you put clothes away and leave the bathroom tidy as well, at least one section of the home isn't shrieking *'don't let anyone come in here – it's a mess!'* It seems obvious once you get into the habit of it, but many people live with messy bedrooms and frequently unmade beds. (The same principle applies in every other room of the house – bottom line: **put away as you go**.)

If we're tidy, not only do we get the benefits, but we also become a role model for our children.

LESSON 49:

Treat it like a job

Picture this:

It's 6:30 in the evening. The kids are fed, bathed and in their pyjamas. Their homework is done. Their uniforms (clean and ironed) are hanging on their wardrobe doors, ready for tomorrow morning. School bags are packed and lunches are made, keeping fresh overnight in the fridge.

An impossible dream? Actually, no! My friend Kate Booker spent some years as a nanny and routinely achieved this scenario with up to four kids by knock-off time at 6:30pm every evening.

It is possible, but it does take practice, planning, discipline... and a little bit of luck!

The key is to set a major deadline (for example the scenario above) and then break the afternoon up into smaller milestones.

Kate's after-school routine

- *Home from school, out of school uniform and finish afternoon tea by 3:45pm.*
- *Kids play, you prepare dinner and do ironing (if you haven't gone the wrinkle-free path with all your clothes) until 4:30pm.*
- *Finish homework and school bags packed by 5:00pm.*
- *Finish dinner by 5:45pm.*
- *Finish bath by 6:15pm.*

Although this sounds very regimented, it's important to remember that children's lives at school are quite strictly time-tabled. You don't need to ring a bell to get things moving; just keep an eye on your watch and let them know when it's time to move on from one activity to another.

By setting mini-milestones, you know when you're starting to run late and you'll need to move things along in order to make your deadline. For example, if you're still doing homework by 5:15pm, you'll need to speed up dinner and bath time (perhaps give the kids a shower instead).

The other key to achieving nanny-like efficiency is to remember all the things a parent does that are outside a nanny's job description, and relegate them to another time. Stick to the job at hand and leave tasks like personal phone calls, cleaning the house, arranging tradespeople and the like to another time when you'll be more effective and they won't interfere with the afternoon routine.

With the example above, obviously a parent or caregiver is in the house with the children straight after school. The routine will be different if children are in after-school care and everyone arrives home together, but the basic premise still stands; chunk out the elements of the routine and aim not to get side-tracked on to other tasks. It's a basic time-management skill.

LESSON 50:

Homework tricks and tips

Homework can become one of the most testing activities of the day, leading to tears of frustration, raised voices and notes home from school.

As a nanny, Kate's approach was to take time out from other activities such as preparing dinner to give the young children her full and undivided attention until it was done.

'By that time of the day they were tired, their attention was waning and the last thing they felt like doing was more school work. Homework was taking over an hour with me nagging them while I tried to get my other chores done in between interruptions.

'I discovered that if I sat with them, it kept their momentum and attention levels high and we were done in less than half the time. It was far more time- and energy-efficient in the long run, not to mention much more pleasant for everyone!'

This can become difficult when you have younger children who have no homework and who are busily (and noisily) playing in the background. Kate's solution was to apply a rule that during homework time all the kids sat at the table in the family room with paper and pencils. The pre-schoolers drew pictures or looked at picture books while the school-age children did their homework.

'Apart from keeping distractions to a minimum, littlies actually feel like it's a game. They're playing at being a big kid and doing homework. Also, you're instituting good habits in them while they're very young instead of sending a message that homework is a punishment that stops you having fun.'

Another of her tips

'A parent or carer is not there to do homework for a child, but to mentor or coach them. In school classes of 30 or so, children get very little one-on-one attention.

'I like the model of a sporting coach who will sit with a protégé through each exercise, encouraging them and telling them what to do next. Children respond to your leadership and will start to model their behaviour on yours. If you assist them with homework problems and assignments, they will start to mimic and adopt the problem-solving techniques you use.'

LESSON 51:

Do it the night before

By the end of the day, all most parents can think of is bed. You know that moment when suddenly you can barely drag one leg after the other? To add in one more task – laying things out for the morning to save the madhouse effect as the herd stampedes to school, kindergarten or childcare – seems just too hard.

Step back and have another think. What concurrent activity can you or the children do earlier in the evening?

Perhaps whoever dries the dishes or unloads the dishwasher could set the table for breakfast after dinner is cleared away. (Of course that depends on whether you use the table for other activities such as homework, and where the table is. If lounge and dining room are one, and you do manage a few minutes of tranquillity before bed, you may not want reminders of tomorrow in your vision.)

Make lunches while you prepare the dinner. Or, you might even make a week's worth in one go. (See the following section on food for more on this topic.)

Ironing shirts, sewing on buttons, packing the school bags, finding a mysteriously vanished pair of trainers or pantyhose without a hole are all night-before jobs. Wait until the morning and you'll be stressed before you get out the door.

LESSON 52:

Making laundry less of a chore

These excellent laundry-related tips come courtesy of some faithful blog/ezine readers.

- **Simplify linen changing:** *If you are not putting the freshly washed sheets, duvet covers and pillow cases straight back on the beds, fold them all up and put them into one pillow case per bed. This way, all you need to grab out of the linen cupboard is the full pillowcase.*

- **Laundromats:** *Consider using a laundromat rather than your home drier over winter. You can dry eight to 10 loads in 40 minutes in a commercial drier, it costs about $6, is much easier on your clothes and far quicker. You can then just have one giant folding session a week (or get the laundromat to fold for you), your power costs are kept down and you don't have the dampness in your home from running the drier –* **Lisa Rose,** *who is a Mother of 6.*

- **Don't fold what's not necessary:** *Flannels and bibs don't need to be folded – throw them all together into a drawer or a bin in a cupboard –* **Karen.**

- **Soaking stains away:** *I kept a bucket of water and pre-mixed laundry powder (or Napisan) in the laundry and put soiled bibs/shorts/socks/tea towels straight into it. By the time I washed them, the stains had soaked themselves away. No scrubbing, stain remover or bleaching –* **Catherine**, *who had four children in the space of six years.*

- **Multiple washing baskets:** *Purchase mesh washing baskets from the $2 shop, and place about the house. This seems to encourage the girls (now aged 2 – 7) to manage their own washing, or at least keep it off the floor and not mixed with clean stuff –* **Colette**.

- **Bathroom:** *Have a different colour set of towels for each person in* the family. It's then very obvious if someone hasn't hung up their towel.

- **Laundry:** Once children are old enough – from about four years old - let them sort their washing into three baskets (white, blacks and coloured) to assist with laundry day. Once they are older teach them to load the washing machine –**Diane Lithgow**.

- **A sock box:** If you want to match your socks then do it yourself. Why do we have to wear matching stuff anyway? – **Heather**.

SECTION V:

FAST AND HEALTHY FOOD – YES, YOU CAN HAVE BOTH!

LESSON 53:

Simplify your grocery shopping

Grocery shopping is one of those tasks we all have to do – and it's a time-consumer. You might have already switched to buying your groceries online, in which case you can feel very clever. For many years I put off the change. It was justified by the fact that my schedule varies greatly and no two weeks are the same. However, two experiences a couple of weeks apart gave me the kick in the butt I needed.

The first prompt was delivered by a two-year old.

I was babysitting three of my granddaughters for a few days. This included my youngest grandchild of not quite two. Monday came and the weather was reasonable so Brianna and Olivia carefully rode their bikes to school while I pushed the toddler in her stroller. Once the big girls were safely delivered I decided to pop into the nearby supermarket for a few supplies.

All was well until I slowed down in the wine department, looking for a particular brand of Pinot Noir. Little Bethany started to wriggle and then stood up. Practicing a potential future career as a ballerina, her pointed toes waved over the metal frame of the pushchair. Smiling fondly at her, I freed my wee poppet from her pushchair. She couldn't go far, I thought.

I was wrong! And if you're a parent used to shopping with little ones, you'll be shaking your head at my naivety.

Not more than a minute later, having found the bottle I was after, I looked up. No toddler in sight! Yikes! My blood pressure instantly skyrocketed.

For the next five minutes I sprinted around the aisles, becoming increasingly worried. A couple of local mothers who knew the family had spotted us together and joined in the search.

First stop was the door leading to the busy carpark. Thankfully there was no blonde head prancing around the backs of any cars. Phew!

Back to the aisles.

Suddenly I was flooded with relief. Here was my little escapee, cheerily wandering toward me with a very nice-looking cheese to go with the wine.

Reminder to self: There's no such thing as a 'quick and easy' shopping experience with small children.

Use someone else's time and petrol

The second experience happened on my doorstep.

After a busy day with clients in the city I'd diverted off the motorway to a nearby supermarket to get supplies. I'd left town before the traffic got too heavy but by the time I'd done my shopping, evening rush-hour madness had erupted.

As a result, that one 'quick' visit to the supermarket had taken close to an extra hour on an already long day.

Finally – home. I was wearily unloading the groceries when a small truck turned into the next-door driveway. It was a delivery from the supermarket I'd just been at! My neighbour works from home, and the only time she had invested in her grocery shopping was a few minutes on her computer and to greet the delivery man at her front door.

Guess what I've registered for now!

Buy in bulk

Country people have traditionally bulk shopped – a trip to town is carefully planned. If you live 100 kilometres from the nearest grocery store you don't pop down the road every couple of days. (Or if you do, you're either working in town or you're a very poor planner!)

Even if you live close to shops, bulk buying is a time-saver. You may have to re-arrange your cupboards to store a month's supplies, but it's worth it to save on time and vehicle expenses, let alone the challenges of going shopping with small children. Monthly bulk-buying of non-food items such as cleaning products and toilet paper is easy and lets you make the most of items on special.

If you are doing your shopping online, you'll spend less time placing the order and unpacking if you do it every fortnight or month. All those minutes count.

A tip from Lisa on bulk supplies

Make sure you have enough cans in your cupboard, meat in your freezer and other basic supplies, to be able to produce a meal at a moment's notice without having to shop. If my canned tomatoes get below six in the cupboard, I start to get nervous.

If you have the freezer space, freeze spare bottles of milk rather than having to buy more during the week – **Lisa Rose**.

Consider a 'chosen for you' food service

These are becoming more popular and provide a great service if you don't even want to think about choices. The full-meal services come with menus, recipes and all ingredients. There are also fruit and vegetable services that deliver to your door. Caution: the 'chosen for you' services might be a bit more expensive, although there is little waste if you're at home most nights.

More readers' tips

The shopping list

I go through the house diary and put one large Post-it in for each week. On there all family members write groceries items that are needed as they run out. I then take the Post-it to the supermarket and put it on the handle of the trolley as I shop.

No more scraps of paper. The list is all in one place and I don't have to try and hold a list as I push the trolley. I have had lots of positive comments from other shoppers about it – **Sarah**.

Pre-prepared shopping list to save time and money

I have made an A4 page shopping list for our local supermarket. The items are listed roughly in the order I come to them as I go around the supermarket. This allows me to whizz around quicker than most people.

The list also has a column for an estimated price, which we note when an item is added to the list. This is a huge help with sticking to our budget.

I keep spare sheets in my recipe book. Each week I place one shopping list on the fridge and as grocery items run out the list is filled in accordingly. Then, when I plan my weekly menu I add the rest of the items that are required for the week.

As I go around the supermarket I've had numerous people comment on my list and I've even had people ask for a copy of it, which I've always happily emailed to them. It doesn't have all the items at the supermarket but it has the ones that our family uses the most. Every now and then as the family requirements change I modify the list, but I've only done that a few times in the past five – six years.

If items aren't put on the shopping list then the family usually misses out until the next week; they've now learnt to take responsibility for putting things on the list as they run out.

I've been using this for many years now and it definitely saves time and money! – **Louise**.

LESSON 54:

Never skip breakfast

However late you're running, however much they protest, don't let your kids skip breakfast and don't skip breakfast yourself. Studies show that children who skip breakfast have less energy and perform worse at school. (The same goes for adults, of course.) What's more, everyone will be more tired and ratty when they get home in the evening. Skipping breakfast also makes you more inclined to over-eat later in the day and make bad food choices when you're hungry.

If you're in a hurry, make sure you always have some nutritious food on hand for high-speed emergency exits and consumption in the car, bus or train. A packet of wholegrain or rice crackers, a bag of almonds or fresh fruit are an easy backup.

Quick and healthy breakfast ideas
- Cereal and milk. Even young children can get their own breakfast if you lay out the packets, spoons and bowls the night before and put the milk where they can reach it in the fridge.
- Muesli. Ideally, make your own without all the additives that give the commercial versions a longer shelf life.
- Fresh fruit.
- Wholemeal grainy toast.
- Yoghurt – choose natural Greek varieties that aren't packed with sugar.
- Muesli bars (for the *'really* running late' days!) Read the labels carefully when you shop – most bars are very high in sugar. Don't be fooled by the health claims on the packaging.

LESSON 55:

Keep their energy up!

Did you know all humans need some 'brain food' every three hours? For long-lasting energy, it is best to combine carbohydrates with fats and proteins. Carbohydrates on their own will cause your blood sugar levels to spike then sky dive, leaving you feeling hungry again. This sort of eating increases the risk of Type 2 diabetes.

It's very important to eat a wide variety of whole fibre-rich natural foods, rather than highly-processed alternatives laden with sugar, fat and salt.

Examples

Combine one option from column A with one from column B for a balanced meal or snack.

High Carbohydrate	High Protein
Wholegrain crackers	Cheese
Carrot sticks	Cottage cheese
Grainy bread	Vegemite/Marmite
Celery sticks	Peanut butter
Wholemeal wrap	Salmon
Potato or kumara (sweet potato)	Boiled egg
Rice wafer	Tuna
Muesli	Nuts
Fruit/Dried fruit	Seeds
Fruit salad	Natural yoghurt

You can not only improve your kids' alertness and energy levels at school, but set yourself up for a less crazy afternoon if you and the children eat some carbohydrate, paired together with protein and/or healthy fat, at least every three hours throughout the day. Also, remember that eating regular brain food will mean you're less likely to make poor choices when you do eat.

If the children have a long trip home or after-school sport or other activities, pack a post-school snack to keep their energy levels up until dinner time.

Great sports people eat well

LESSON 56:

Slow cooker

Do you have a crockpot or slow cooker? They're a wonderful kitchen tool.

Before you head out for the day, throw a cheap cut of meat with some vegetables into a crockpot and you'll dine like a king in the evening.

If you're strapped for time in the morning prepare everything the night before and leave it in the fridge until morning. It will only take a minute or two to load and switch on the pot.

Apart from the joy of knowing dinner is waiting as you walk in the door, the wonderful aroma that greets you is its own reward. Pavlov's dog salivating at the sound of a bell has nothing on the taste buds activated by the inviting smell of a waiting hot meal.

Margaret's innovative way to use up left-over vegetables

- *Once a week, before shopping, clean out the vegetable bin of your fridge. Put anything that looks a bit limp and unappetising through the food processor to make soup.*
- *Place the ground-up vegetables in the crock pot, adding a cereal soup mix if you like.*
- *Use some right away and put the rest in meal-sized portions in the freezer.*
- *Alternatively, any glass jars with sealable lids can be used as preserving jars. Just put the soup in hot, and check that the seal clicks down as it cools.*

And there you are – clean fridge, no waste and there's always a quick and healthy meal in your freezer or pantry. **Margaret Lyall**.

LESSON 57:

Lunches

Sandwiches, cookies and fruit are the regular fare for lunches, but don't forget the opportunities with left-overs or extras from the night before. If you're cooking something that can be easily portable, consider making extra for tomorrow's lunch. Baked vegetables, lasagne, stew with rice or meat loaf are just four possibilities.

And what about salads? (The children might not want salads for lunch, but you have to eat too!) As you prepare a salad for the night before, make extra for lunch. Take the dressing in a separate container to add just before eating.

Tip

Dish straight into the lunch containers as you serve dinner – otherwise the lunch portions might just disappear into roving gullets.

Sandwiches

Save your time and sanity by making a week's worth of lunches in one go and freezing them. You'll be delighted at how quickly you can make 10 or 15 sandwiches. In the morning, give each child a frozen sandwich for their lunch box. It will be defrosted by lunchtime and often taste fresher than if you'd made it that morning.

If you keep sliced bread in the freezer, you don't even need to defrost it to make the sandwiches. Simply butter the frozen slices, add the toppings, wrap and re-freeze. If you're interested in reducing the use of plastic, look into bees' wax wraps, or even plain unbleached cotton cloth.

Sandwich toppings that freeze well

- cheese
- ham
- corned beef
- chicken or turkey
- peanut butter

Sandwich-making for the whole family could be a Sunday night chore for older children. Mind you, if you have teenage boys, this tip probably won't work. When my boys were that age I doubt any freezer would have been big enough for a week's worth of prepared lunches! They could devour a whole loaf of bread in a matter of minutes.

Alternatively, get the kids to make their lunch the night before. It saves congestion and fluster at the kitchen bench in the morning.

LESSON 58:

Double batch

As with bulk shopping, this is a wonderful time-saver. While you have everything out on the bench, why cook for only one meal? Double or triple the recipe, put the surplus into the freezer, and you've got meals in the 'bank'.

Then on the nights you're the town taxi with a mob of dirty tired children crammed in after sports training, or you've worked late, or you're just plain exhausted, voilà – a nutritious and inexpensive dinner is only a few microwave minutes away.

Back in my days of feeding the 5,000 (believe me, it felt like it at times!) we were somewhat more random. If there were any left-overs (once the boys were teenagers there was no such thing!) they'd be popped in the fridge for recycling that week. Occasionally I would double-batch biscuits or a cake, but I rarely did it for dinners. I wish I'd thought of doing double-batch dinners; it would have saved hours.

For in-depth easy-to-read strategies on the topic and heaps of great recipes I strongly recommend *Real Food Less Fuss* by my daughter-in-law Lauren Parsons.

Until you can get your hands on Lauren's book (see the Resources section), I've extracted a few pointers for you:

- *Plan meals that freeze well.*
- *Have sufficient equipment to prepare and cook bigger amounts. Is your mixing bowl big enough? Do you have several loaf tins for meat loaves? Or enough easily stackable containers to freeze the extra meals?*
- *Have a permanent marker and labels in the kitchen.*

- *Set aside the surplus meals before you dish out that night's dinner and don't let the vultures raid them for seconds (or thirds, or fourths.)*
- *Don't put hot meals straight in the fridge or freezer. Once they've stopped steaming, put them in the fridge, and then into the freezer once they're chilled.*
- *Label each one with the name and date of production.*
- *Although a frozen meal can quickly be defrosted in the microwave, try to plan ahead by taking the meal out of the freezer in the morning. It will minimise the nagging from hungry grizzling kids if you've all walked in the door together, or the risk of appetites being spoiled by snacking just before food is on the table. This applies to adults as well as children. If you're endeavouring to reach or keep a healthy weight, pre-dinner snacks are a major trap. When we're hungry and tired, our resistance to impulse snacking is low.*
- *If you want to be really organised and regularly double-batch, record each meal as you put it away. A small whiteboard fastened to the freezer door is easy to maintain. Don't forget to update when you take a meal out.*
- *To really enhance the meal, whip up a quick fresh salad and eat this as a first course before your main meal (think French style entrée). This greatly boosts your nutrition, slows down your entire meal and leaves you feeling much more satisfied overall.*
- *Something frozen doesn't look as appetising when you take it out of the freezer. Remember to garnish it with different coloured vegetables and herbs when you plate it for the family. Our appetites are greatly impacted by what our eyes see.*

LESSON 59:

Consider feeding younger children early

Dinner time is sometimes the only time the family sits down together as a group, but if you find it's the most stressful time of day, consider feeding small children on their own. This allows you and your partner to sit down alone to dinner and have some grown-up talk after the darlings are in bed, rather than coaxing and coercing while your own meal gets cold.

If they've had their main dinner early, you can have some family together time by playing a board game, reading out loud, or sitting down together later in the evening for a dessert. As the kids will have already had their main meal they won't be fractious, and if they don't eat, it doesn't matter. A dessert can be something healthy such as a tub of yoghurt or some fresh or tinned fruit.

Kids can be unadventurous with their diet, so don't fight it all the time. A repertoire of a few simple meals for those 'too tired' nights will give them enough variety and save your sanity.

Nine easy kid-friendly meals for when you're exhausted

1. Boiled egg and toast.
2. Cheese and tomato on toast.
3. Baked beans or spaghetti with a poached egg.
4. Scrambled eggs.
5. A 'platter dinner' – with mini sandwiches, salami stick, cheese, fruit, crackers.
6. Toasted sandwiches, including BLT – bacon, lettuce, tomato sandwich.

7. Tinned soup with toast or crackers.
8. Spaghetti, butter and parmesan cheese or a tinned sauce.
9. Breakfast cereal and milk. (It won't kill them once in a while!)

On the other hand ...

... an alternative point of view is discussed in **Lesson 19:** *What we can learn from the French about raising children.*

You might apply both techniques at different times, depending on your energy levels. For example, another idea is to make Saturday night family-dinner night or to institute a family breakfast on Sunday mornings. Meals together are great for instilling good manners, sharing what's been happening in each person's world, and building strong relationships.

Another of Heather's tips: Family meals

Once a day we all sit down to eat together. There are so many benefits but we also use a bit of this time to update family members on activities, who is in or out on certain days, things we've achieved.

The older the kids have got, the more valuable this has become. We eat later as a consequence so I allow a small, healthy snack in the evening. The benefit definitely outweighs the inconvenience – **Heather Douglas.**

LESSON 60:

The battle of the vegetables

Two of my inspirations around this whole topic of feeding children quality food are Pamela Druckerman's book *Bringing up Bébé* and Lauren Parsons' *Real Food Less Fuss*, which I've already mentioned. It's no coincidence that both have been influenced by the French way of cooking and eating.

Kids often prefer raw vegetables to cooked ones. Try offering sticks of carrot or celery with some hummus or a mild yoghurt dip (such as tzatziki), or even a cup of frozen peas.

Disguise the vegetables

My niece Jody disguises the vegetables in a big batch of meat sauce – mince, kidney beans, every vegetable she can find, pasta sauce and tinned tomatoes. Once cooked, everything is blended so all the vegies are hidden. It is then frozen in meal-sized amounts. Serve with a quick green salad, pasta or rice and you've got a healthy meal in 10 minutes.

Salad entrée first

Another of Lauren's tips for getting vegetables into the troops came from her year of living in France as an exchange student. It's now an integral part of her advice and I've observed how effective it is.

Start with a salad or fresh vegetable entrée of some kind – with nothing else on the table. It might be a simple green salad, or it could be two or three vegetables, often garnished with herbs and mixed together with a vinaigrette dressing. Her book has a whole section of Sensational Salad Blueprints, and you'll find a couple of her recipes for vinaigrette on the next pages.

Think of colour, taste and texture. Make it interesting but keep it fast and easy to prepare. You can make a very tasty salad with only two ingredients and a nice home-made dressing.

The salad comes while everyone is still hungry. The meat (or other protein if you're vegetarian), the rest of the vegetables, and any carbohydrate accompaniment – potato, rice, couscous or pasta – don't appear until the first course has gone.

Examples

- Grated carrot and sultanas.
- Lettuce and watercress with a light sprinkling of pine nuts, sesame seeds or pumpkin kernels.
- Lightly steamed green beans tossed with feta cheese.
- Beetroot and feta.
- Basil and tomato dressed with a good quality olive oil.
- Cucumber, red onion and tomato.
- Diced carrot, apple, cucumber, cherry tomatoes and cubed cheese. Most kids love this one.

When first introducing kids to vegetables, start with the 'sweeter' varieties such as carrot, red capsicum, cucumber, sweet peas and cherry tomatoes. Later on, you can add beans, broccoli, leafy greens and other vegetables that are rich in important vitamins and minerals.

Lauren's classic fresh French vinaigrette recipe, learned while living in France

- A grind of salt and pepper
- 1-2 tsp mustard
- 2 Tbsp red wine vinegar
- 3 Tbsp extra virgin olive oil

The traditional way to prepare this (which also saves on the washing up) is to mix your vinaigrette directly in the bottom of your salad bowl before adding the salad ingredients.

- Mix together the mustard, vinegar, salt and pepper until well combined.
- Note that it is best to mix this before adding the oil as the acid (vinegar in this case) helps the other ingredients to combine properly.
- Add the oil gradually, while mixing well.
- Add salad ingredients and turn it all together gently to coat everything evenly.

Vinaigrette in a jar

What I recommend as a time saver is to mix up a larger quantity of vinaigrette in a jar to last you for a week or two. Simply store the jar in the fridge and shake it each time before serving. You can then pour or spoon out two to four tablespoons onto your salad, depending on the size, and mix it all well until everything is coated.

To make your classic vinaigrette in a jar simply combine:

- 3-4 Tbsp mustard
- 2/3 cup acid, e.g. red wine vinegar, balsamic vinegar, apple cider vinegar, lemon or lime juice
- 1 cup oil, e.g. extra virgin olive oil, avocado oil, macadamia oil
- ½-1 tsp each salt and pepper

The varieties are endless as you can use any sort of acid and any sort of oil in the ratio two parts acid to three parts oil. Varying the types of acids and oils you use will give you slightly different styles of vinaigrette. Try out different mustards, and add in extra flavour such as honey or spices as well.

[reprinted with permission from Lauren Parsons, Real Food Less Fuss, 2016. Available at www.RealFoodLessFuss.com]

LESSON 61:

Try taking something away from them

My aunt and uncle were looking after their grandson Tony for about a week. They'd been warned that he was a fussy eater and decided to take the line of least resistance, leaving the parents to work on his eating habits while they just enjoyed having a small child to entertain.

One night Brussels sprouts were on the menu.

'Do you like Brussels sprouts?' Peggy asked.

'No, I hate them.'

So Peggy didn't put any on his plate.

As they sat down to eat, Tony looked at the adult plates, then at his plate and his face dropped.

'What's the matter, Tony?' asked his grandfather.

'I want the little cabbages too,' was the plaintive response.

He gobbled them all up and asked for more. For the next week Brussels sprouts became the green vegetable of choice.

Along the same line of reverse psychology is Lauren Child's Charlie and Lola picture book *I Will Never Not Ever Eat a Tomato*. You'll find the YouTube version at www.youtube.com/watch?v=0Vd-0pFOFs0. Neither you nor your irritatingly stubborn loved ones will ever think of carrots – sorry, orange twiglets from Jupiter – or peas, potatoes or tomatoes, in the same way again.

LESSON 62:

Use quality condiments to make food tasty

I can't move on from this topic without a quick note on condiments, dressings and salt from a foodie perspective, based on my observations of everyday French family cuisine.

The first step is to make sure your condiments, as well as your ingredients, are fresh and tasty. A few basic quality items are a far better use of money than a pantry full of stale old herbs and spices, and rancid dressings and oils.

I realise some families cannot afford anything but the basics when it comes to food, and every week it's a struggle to stretch the budget around the voracious fridge-raiders. However, if you are interested in extending your child's palate as well as preparing and enjoying simple, healthy and delicious food, you might like to consider a couple of 'luxuries' – they're not expensive if used correctly.

Choose a quality oil

Extra virgin olive oil is the highest quality olive oil and a very effective dressing by itself. Do not confuse it with low-grade adulterated and chemically processed olive oil and don't waste it as a cooking oil.

- Buy it in a dark-coloured bottle or a tin. It's affected by sunlight.
- Choose cold-pressed virgin olive oil, as recently bottled or canned as possible.
- Try to buy only what you'll use within six months.
- If you've had it for a while, do a sniff and taste test. Oil will go rancid – and spoil your good food.

All salt is not created equal

Great salt accents the flavour of your food. Try sprinkling it with a high quality rock or sea salt, available at all the good foodie places. My personal favourite is a French one – Fleur du Sal de Guérande, perhaps because I've been there and seen the method of production. It's hand-harvested by *paludiers* (salt marsh workers) from Southern Brittany. *Délicieux!*

In ancient times, salt was a very expensive item – wars were fought over it. Even today quality salts are significantly more expensive than your regular common or garden machine-produced variety. However, you only use a small amount.

Tip: Don't leave it by the stove where some ill-informed person might add it to the cooking. I hide mine when I can't control what's going on in my kitchen! (Translate that to mean teenagers and adults who haven't been inducted into the joys of French-style cooking.)

LESSON 63:

Pre-planning menus

Plan your meals for the week and you'll reduce costs, save time and never need to eat takeaways unless it's by choice.

Here are eight of the 11 principles Lauren Parsons shares in *Real Food Less Fuss*. I've deliberately not given you all 11. If time-efficient healthy eating is of interest to you, I really urge you to get the book.

1. Plan your week.
2. Work your plan.
3. Display your menu.
4. Shop to your menu.
5. Simplify your shopping.
6. Fresh is always first.
7. Never waste food.
8. Enjoy a weekly cook-up.

She begins her planning chapter with the following advice:

'Plan your menu for each week in advance to suit your lifestyle. On the nights when you know you will be home late or have limited time, plan a quick and easy ten minute dinner, a meal that cooks itself or a 'twice as nice' defrosted meal.'

The whole chapter is jammed full of practical how-to tips. It's a very worthwhile investment.

SECTION VI:

A FEW OBSERVATIONS ON TECHNOLOGY OVER-USE

LESSON 64:

Turn off your phone – create a 'no contact' zone

Maybe we need to start a Tech-aholics Anonymous! The problem is that technology is fun, easy, alluring and yes… addictive. It's wonderful to be able to instantly connect with people anywhere – but do we need to do it all the time? What are the consequences to our personal relationships?

You might like to ponder these questions

- Is it OK to ignore those you're with if something more interesting (or attention-grabbing) intrudes?
- If you're a parent, what are you teaching your children about priorities?
- When was the last time you switched off your phone and just 'hung out' with a child?

One downside of our digital world is the risk of superficiality – and that includes our personal relationships as well as our business ones.

Case study

Two close friends had lived in the same Australian city for some years, until one of them moved to the United States. A couple of years later they both attended a conference in the US so decided that rooming together would be a great way to reconnect.

Following the conference, one of them described to me what happened.

'I was so looking forward to spending time with Vanessa. But whenever we were in our room together and finally had time to talk

without others around, she spent all her time on her phone checking Facebook and other social media. I came home feeling ignored, sad and really let down. I feel as though I'm not important to her anymore.'

If you think you might be falling into the tech-guilt trap, try getting family agreement to turn all digital devices off when you're spending quality time together. You might be surprised at the results.

Another idea

Every now and then you might like to pretend you're in a no-signal and no-power phone area. Turn off the phone, tablet or other device. Don't turn on the computer. Let everyone's brains defrag!

LESSON 65:

Make meal times device-free

Some families have a basket near the table and all devices are turned off or to silent and placed in the basket before family members take their seats at any meal.

A great cultural example of phone management

A significant feature of French family life is the importance placed on sharing meals. It's a time to share the highlights of the day, discuss events, and simply be together. I've never seen a mobile phone in evidence at any of my French friends' tables, except when we were using it as a translation tool to help communicate, or sharing clever tech ideas and apps. To take a call while with others is regarded as the height of disrespect and rudeness. (That's not to say that some French people don't over-use their mobiles, but the smart ones certainly set boundaries.)

The focus instead is on savouring the food, enjoying the conversation, and relaxing with people they care about.

Let's copy the French and make our meals a time to be fully present with the people at our table.

LESSON 66:

A creative way for technology to be your friend

One weekend I had the joy of looking after three grandsons while their parents were off at an agricultural conference.

On the Saturday morning I was chatting to a mother on the side-line of seven-year-old Matt's first rugby game for the season. *'My son struggles to keep up,'* she said, pointing to the chubby lad lagging at the back of the pack. *'I've been telling him he needs to do some runs to get a bit fitter and faster.'*

At a guess, he spent a lot more time sitting down than his lean and healthy team mates, most of whom were farm kids. I suspect TV and possibly computers or Xbox-type devices were his most likely entertainment. I realise this might sound harsh, but as you'll read in the next lesson, studies by Aric Sigman have made a direct correlation between screen time and obesity/health issues.

'Once he gets into the weekly practice I'm sure he'll tone up,' I said reassuringly. And then, wanting to give her some helpful suggestions instead of just platitudes, I added: *'My grandsons are on the run all the time. They don't have a TV so outside fun is a regular part of their day. Plus, they're constantly looking for ways to earn computer dollars, which helps keep them moving as well.'*

I *think* she heard the bit about running around but what really got her attention was the computer dollars.

'What are they?' she said with interest, once she'd recovered from the shock of a family with no TV.

Computer dollars

I explained that it was a great way to teach them responsibility for jobs around the house and at the same time to ensure that computer usage was kept at a reasonable level.

'The two older boys are seven and nine,' I told her. *'They're not paid for routine tasks such as picking up their toys, but for most other chores they negotiate with their parents about how many 'dollars' they can earn. One 'dollar' earns five minutes on the computer. Even the four year old earns a computer dollar if he makes his bed – usually that just means pulling up the duvet.'*

Earning opportunities for these small boys

- Tie or untie the dogs and feed them: $1
- Stack/unstack the dishwasher: $1
- Clean the basins and mirrors in both bathrooms: $2
- Mow the lawn: $4 (the seven-year-old was the main lawnmower man at the time)
- Sweep the garage: $2
- Vacuum the whole house: $6

The other big benefit is the entrepreneurship they're learning by osmosis – they go looking for jobs so they can earn computer time. When I hear a child ask: *'Please can I clean the bathroom?'* I know these clever parents are onto something.

And a side benefit is the maths practice. As I write this book, the computer dollar has now upped in value – it's worth six minutes on the computer instead of five. The boys are pretty good on their five times tables and now it's time to consolidate the six times tables.

Here's Matt at seven doing a very good job on his favourite task. I *think* he likes to mow, but he *certainly* likes the computer time he earns!

LESSON 67:

How is screen time impacting your children?

Years ago, people working in the television industry told me that there is a direct inverse relationship between the amount of TV a person watches – and these days we would include any devices providing entertainment – and the income they're capable of earning. In other words, those who spend a lot of time being entertained by external sources are not stimulating their creative brain and will not be capable of generating higher income. Whether this has been proven by robust studies, I do not know, but it's worth some consideration.

Of course, our present or future income-earning capabilities are only one facet of the issue. What about the children?

What is screen time doing to our kids' brains?

There's a huge amount of research to show that screen-time distorts and damages children's brains. It's been established that growing children need to develop sustained attention or concentration. Screen-time, even if it's used for education, cultivates the opposite – divided attention.

Consider this: 80% of brain-growth occurs from birth to three years. That's when most of the brain's connections are formed. The French government prohibits French television channels from airing any TV programmes – educational or otherwise – aimed at children under three years of age. The Belgian and US governments also have initiatives in place or recommendations to stop children under three from seeing any screen media. And New Zealand Ministry of Health experts, as recently as 2016, recommend that children under two should have no screen time, while for older children screen time should be limited to less than an hour a day.

If you're at all concerned about the impact of screen-time on young children, I strongly encourage you to look into the work of internationally respected psychologist Dr Aric Sigman, author of *Remotely Controlled – How Television is Damaging Our Lives*.

Here are some excerpts from his work, mainly his scholarly article *Time for a View on Screen Time*. The emphasis is mine.

'In Britain today, children by the age of 10 years have regular access to an average of five different screens at home. In addition to the main family television, for example, many very young children have their own bedroom TV along with portable handheld computer game consoles (e.g., Nintendo, PlayStation, Xbox), smartphone with games, internet and video, a family computer, a laptop and/or a tablet computer (e.g. iPad). Children routinely engage in two or more forms of screen viewing at the same time, such as TV and laptop. Viewing is starting earlier in life. Nearly one in three American infants has a TV in their bedroom, and almost half of all infants watch TV or DVDs for nearly 2 h/day.

'Across the industrialised world, watching screen media is the main pastime of children. Over the course of childhood, children spend more time watching TV than they spend in school. When including computer games, internet and DVDs, by the age of seven years a child born today will have spent one full year of 24 h days watching screen media. **By the age of 18 years, the average European child will have spent 3 years of 24 h days watching screen media**; at this rate, by the age of 80 years, they will have spent 17.6 years glued to media screens.'

His lengthy article then goes on to expand on the health impact of these rather alarming figures. Here's a partial summary of the most salient points. Read his full article for the complete list of studies and research notes; you'll find it listed in the Resources section of this book.

- *There is a highly significant dose-response association between screen time (ST) and risk of Type 2 diabetes, cardiovascular disease (CVD) and all-cause mortality among adults.*

- *Increased TV viewing has been consistently shown to be linked to increased body mass index (BMI) in both children and adults. The association appears stronger in young children.*
- *Preschool children who watch more TV are fatter and less active.*
- *Video game-playing was found to significantly increase food intake in adolescents immediately after playing 'and was not compensated for during the rest of the day.'*
- *A randomised controlled clinical intervention trial divided 4- to 7-year-olds into two groups: one had its TV and computer viewing reduced by half; the other did not. After three years, there had been a significant reduction in the BMI of those who had halved their screen viewing, and relatively little in those who had not.*

Have you ever wondered why there's an increasing number of morbidly overweight people in every Western country? This has to be a significant part of the story. They're spending too much time sitting on their backsides.

Suggestions for managing screen-time

- *Restrict viewing to two half-hour programmes per night per child.*
- *Have a TV-free night once a week.*
- *Use a programme guide to decide what you want to watch, rather than channel surfing.*
- *Parents should be encouraged to monitor and control the time their children spend on hand-held computer games/media.*
- *Ideal discretionary ST limits are:*
    - *3–7 years: 0.5–1 h/day*
    - *7–12 years: 1 h*
    - *12–15 years: 1.5 h*
    - *16+ years: 2 h*
- *Consider how much time your children spend doing homework on computers before deciding on discretionary ST for your child.*

- *Recognise the role modelling influence your own viewing habits have on your children, along with the potential influence of background or 'passive' media.*
- *Schools should adopt a position on the amount of time children spend in front of a screen both at and outside school, and communicate this to pupils and parents.*

[Excerpted with permission from Aric Sigman. 'Time for a View on Screen Time'.]

You might want to do a quick analysis. How many hours are consumed by screen time in your home? And how much time do your children spend in play, sport and other non-screen activities?

SECTION VII:
RAISING TEENAGERS WITHOUT PULLING YOUR HAIR OUT

Coping with teenagers is a huge topic. Here you'll find just a few of my experiences and observations, and also contributions from friends whose philosophies I respect.

LESSON 68:

Time to leave home, sunshine!

My daughter Catherine continued to live at home for another year after she started her university studies. She was a busy young woman, always profitably engaged. As well as study and shift work in the banquets department of one of the top hotels in the city, she also did gardening, cleaning and babysitting for several neighbours. Her customers regularly raved to me about how much they appreciated her work ethic and reliability.

The part-time jobs were to top up her partially-subsidised fees, cover living costs and generate spending money. Essentially she was putting herself through uni.

Because she was earning reasonable money, her step-father Mike and I decided she could contribute to the household in two ways:

1. $20 per week board, due on Fridays. (It was a token contribution but what you don't pay for, you don't appreciate).
2. Be the weekly house cleaner. (We'd previously paid someone to do it).

She was very happy about the deal and, for a while, everything went along smoothly. But as she took on more and more activities, including helping with a youth group across town in her boyfriend's neighbourhood, we began to hear the following stories at an increasing rate.

The first was:

'I'm a bit short this week, Mum. I'll pay you next week.'

Then there were variations on:

'I've done the bathroom and the ironing but I'll have to do the vacuuming next week. I haven't had time.'

We tolerated these inconsistencies for quite a while. We'd discuss the matter and receive promises to improve. However, the incidents continued. We began to feel taken for granted. It seemed that she was brilliant with other employers but taking the easy path with family. Eventually, we decided enough was enough and came up with a plan with dual benefits – income generation for us and encouragement for Catherine to become a fully independent adult.

At the time we lived in a large house. Downstairs was a spacious, self-contained one-bedroom flat that we rented out. Mike and I weren't on large incomes but with careful management of our resources we were slowly building a modest property portfolio. We decided to move ourselves down to the flat and rent out the attractive sunny three-bedroom top floor of the house. Saving a deposit for the next house was one objective; the second concerned Catherine.

'Sorry dear, but you'll have to go flatting. In a few months we're moving downstairs and there won't be room for you.'

At first, our much loved nearly 19-year old was a bit shocked. Life was good at home, with all the conveniences. However, she embraced the challenge and quite quickly found herself a flat about 25 minutes across town.

The experience was a mixed bag – initially enjoyable, at other times challenging. However, she managed it very maturely and learnt a lot about life along the way.

I've heard of other variations on this theme. One couple, with adult children who wouldn't leave home, left the kids in the house and relocated overseas for a few years. Another couple sold the family home and moved into a small apartment.

I strongly believe that once an adult child is capable of supporting themselves, we weaken them if we let them carry on being 'children'. I fully appreciate that there are variations and exceptions, but in general – with either encouragement or a bit of a shove – the fledglings need to go solo as soon as they're able.

Going flatting

LESSON 69:

Preparing our teens to manage money in the big wide world

'You're doing what to your grandson! You're a tough grandmother,' said one of my sailing mates.

Here's what I'd just explained to him. What do you think?

When he was 18, my oldest grandson Sam asked if he could come and live with me for six months. His parents were on an overseas posting for a year and he'd been boarding with his other grandparents for the first six months. They'd been very good to him but I sensed that all parties were keen to consider a change.

'Sure you can,' I replied, *'and here's the deal. I'll be a grandmother when I need to, but let's think of it as a flatting arrangement as much as possible.'*

We'd been on holiday together over the previous six weeks, three of them travelling to visit the parents in Pennsylvania for Christmas. I'd watched pocket money slip through his fingers, much of it wasted on seductive non-essentials and rubbish such as chips and Coke. While he was someone else's responsibility, it wasn't appropriate for me to interfere, but here was Sam giving me the chance to really help.

Another thing I'd noticed was that there seemed to be no savings habit. I'd been party to a number of hopeful conversations that started along the lines of: *'I really need a computer'*, or *'... a better lens for my camera'*. Then would follow a pregnant and hopeful pause – would the Christmas Fairy (i.e. the listener) stump up with the goods? Saving for big items didn't appear to be on the radar.

What's more, his domestic competency left a lot to be desired. He was an able cook when he wanted to be but tidying up after himself was not a priority. And the bedroom? Hmm!

So here I was, faced with a lovely teenager who'd just paid me the compliment of asking to come and live with me. I figured the best way I could play my small part in equipping him for his rapidly looming future was to help him learn to live independently while still in a safe and supportive environment.

For the previous six months he'd been receiving $50 a week pocket money, paid out of the boarding allowance his parents received and passed on to the other grandparents. From what I'd observed, being dished out pocket money wasn't teaching him anything about budgeting or saving.

Over the dinner table we worked out the following arrangement. He would receive the full dependent-child boarding allowance ($245 per week, paid every two weeks). He would pay me a rent of $70 per week (way below market rates) and a nominal $30 per week for utilities (power, water and internet). He would buy and cook all his own food and whatever money was left over was his for savings, incidentals and anything else. I would invite him to share the occasional meal with me if we were both home, but essentially he was on his own.

He was away for a few days when the first two-weekly payment came in. Once we got back together I asked for my $200.

'Oh, I'll get it for you at the end of the week.'

'No love, it doesn't work like that,' I told him. 'Obligations and rent are always paid first.'

So he went to the cash machine. Sure enough, he'd spent almost all the money.

Solid work in the garden paid for that fortnight's board and he had to feed himself for two weeks on $36! I was highly entertained as we walked around the supermarket, watching him plan how to spin the money out. One very focused young man looked very carefully at prices. Bread, mince and pasta go a long way! (I would never have let him starve, but I also wasn't galloping in to the rescue.)

He then set up an automatic payment to pay his commitments first. Even that was a challenge initially – he accidentally paid me too much at the next pay and had nothing left in his bank account to buy an art book for school.

Back to the shocked fellow sailor, a retired surgeon.

'You're not making him pay board!' he said in disbelief. *'Surely you're pulling my leg! Isn't the role of grandparents to be soft and kind and to spoil their grandchildren?'*

'No way,' I replied. *'How can a young man on the edge of adulthood learn if he's treated like a little kid, with pocket money coming of right, no incentive for saving and someone else (in this case me) making all the fiscal decisions? I see my job as a grandparent to provide a safe and protected environment for him to learn responsibility. I won't let him starve; I'm guiding and teaching him. I know he'll make mistakes – that's how we all learn. He has to be able to manage on his own by the time he leaves school.'*

My philosophy is that we have to be tough to be kind. If we over-protect our young ones, we damage them.

Yvonne Godfrey (more about her soon), backs up my sentiments. Here's her advice:

'Don't be their backstop, their 'get out of trouble' card, their extra credit card facility or bank. You've done your job by getting them to adulthood. Now it's your turn to get your life back and spend your money on yourself.'

See also:

Lesson 9: *Parenting for maturity and independence*

Lesson 70: *A contract for living optimally*

Lesson 76: *Parents are not the bank*

LESSON 70:

A contract for living optimally

My good friend Yvonne Godfrey has contributed some of the tips in this section. She's a specialist in helping teenagers morph into wonderful contributory adults and runs MIOMO (Making It On My Own) specifically for this purpose. Yvonne designed a Living Optimally document to negotiate the potentially troubled waters of helping your beloved teen, still at home, to develop the skills he or she will need in a flatting situation. You can download the document at www.parentingyadults.com/templates/. I strongly recommend you also get a copy of her excellent book *Parenting Yadults*. (See the Resources section for more information.)

Yvonne explains

The Living Optimally *document allows you to take stock of how your family treats one another. Think about the kind of language and behaviour that makes people feel safe and loved and what causes division and insecurity. It's not rocket science – it's obvious and yet we so easily slip into language and behaviour that puts others down. We all become over-familiar and the level of respect and love we show one another deteriorates over time. You can also apply these rules to any of your children's friends who visit.*

The document is simply a template, which you can adapt to suit your family's situation. The purpose of the Living Optimally *document is to set up financial accountability, share the running of the household and to agree on protocols and behaviour within the home.*

To be taken seriously, it needs to be treated like a written contract and signed. Verbal agreements can quickly deteriorate, leaving everyone feeling frustrated. The Living Optimally *contract can be a great catalyst for change as well as a good opportunity for your young one to learn the importance of a binding contract. This may sound a bit over the top, but remember – you're preparing them for the realities of the real world – for where they're going, not for where they are now.*

The contract has to be seen positively and should be fully agreed upon by everyone involved – not one-sided, but a win-win for all. Remember, the contract is a tool to create success and harmony and is never to be used as a weapon for revenge or punishment.

LESSON 71:

Everyone's responsible for their own mess

One of my workshop participants once asked for some tips around getting her messy older kids/teens to tidy up after themselves.

The answer is simple but not easy: make everyone responsible for their own mess, right from a very young age. I suspect this parent had made a rod for her own back years before by not insisting on this.

Earlier in the book we discussed getting young children involved with domestic chores. To recap, even a three-year-old is capable of running their dirty clothes to the laundry basket. Pretty soon they'll be able to hang up the towels. And who said parents are the camels? Very small children can bring their backpacks in from the car, put away their gear, and set the table.

At first it will take longer to get the result you want, but if you keep cleaning up after them, you'll do it until you die. The key is not to expect small children to be perfect. Praise what they can do and don't finish it to your standards unless it's really important, preferably when they're not around to notice.

However, you'll need to keep reinforcing the point even when they're teenagers. And sometimes it's other adults in the house who also need a reminder.

Case Study: Let them learn – and keep out of the way

Have you ever walked into the kitchen and found a mess, yet no-one takes responsibility?

One day, fed up with being the maid, I laid down an ultimatum to my teenage daughter and second husband, *'OK guys, I'm sick of cleaning up after you all. From now on, anything left lying around will be dumped in the bedrooms.'*

For two days no sinful item lurked. Then, the good intentions slipped.

I came home early from work a few days later to find a number of miscellaneous items dotted around the lounge and 10 items decorating the bench, including the baking dish from the previous night's roast. Our family rule was that the cook didn't clean up. The night before I'd prepared the meal and one of the others had been on dishes.

I laid towels on the offenders' bedroom carpets, where they couldn't miss them. For Husband it was on his side of the bed. I deposited the unclaimed items on the relevant towels and shut the doors. Later, when the two guilty parties arrived home from work, I hid my smile and kept out of the way.

A few minutes later grumpy faces and dirty dishes appeared at the sink. Not a word was said but the message was clear. It was never as bad again.

Key points

- Give them prior warning.
- If you promise reprisals, you must follow through.
- Keep calm – don't say anything when you're mad. It doesn't have anything like the same impact as a message delivered calmly and quietly.

Hard as it sometimes is, if we run around being the vacuum cleaner on legs, the picker-upper for everyone else in the family, we not only *don't* teach them good habits, but instead we actively encourage them to be lazy.

Every little assistance helps a busy parent. Most teenagers, and some adults, will revert to mucky pups unless you keep the pressure on.

If we don't teach this vital skill, as adults they'll probably be the inhabitants of messy offices and messy homes and will struggle to be efficient. People are less likely to trust important work to them because they're perceived as disorganised. They're also more likely to suffer stress and a sense of overload – the common complaint of people who feel they've got too much to do.

From a correspondent

When I had young children, I would sort their mess with them when I could. It kept the house looking reasonably tidy and when my house looks tidy I get so much more done. Somehow a tidy house makes me much more productive.

One family's kitchen rule

'If you're in the kitchen, clean it up. If you use it, put it away or into the dishwasher. If the dishwasher has clean dishes and you want to put dirty things in there, empty it. This means no arguing about whose mess is whose, no frustration, always a clean kitchen.

See also:

Lesson 21: *The job is not done until everything is put away*

Lesson 22: *How to teach the kids tidiness*

LESSON 72:

Tidiness of shared and private spaces

Advice from Yvonne Godfrey

If you are a tidy person and a 'cleany', you have probably run around picking up after the family for years. Your obsession with tidiness can be as irritating to your children as their lack of tidiness, hygiene and cleaning skills are to you.

If this sounds familiar, it's time for a discussion about what is most important to each of you. You may need to cut some slack regarding their bedroom; after all, that is their only private space.

There are three main reasons for a parent to go into a teenager's bedroom

1. *To tidy and clean the room, gather washing, change the bed sheets and remove dirty crockery.*
2. *To check up on what is going on in there.*
3. *To visit for a chat.*

Reason number one is completely invalid. It's not the parent's job to be the housemaid – not now, not ever!

Three areas to get agreement on

1. They look after the property they didn't pay for

This means that they change their sheets at least fortnightly to protect the mattress from all that sweat and dead skin.

If they refuse, then I advise you to remove the mattress! I removed the mattresses off the beds of the 'yadults' who lived with us for a week

while we were filmed for an episode of The World's Strictest Parents.
www.youtube.com/watch?v=n9HtihCXfDs

I even made them sleep outside on the first night because they wouldn't comply with my requests. Google the episode with me and enjoy an hour of fun for the whole family!

2. No eating in the bedroom

There are two good reasons not to eat in the bedroom.

Firstly, it is unhygienic, and food invariably gets mashed into the carpet, furnishings and bedding. My eldest daughter didn't have the tidiest bedroom. I once challenged her as to why she left all her clothes on the floor. She told me that it was her 'floordrobe' and she was keeping the carpet warm! That's not all that was keeping the carpet warm. When we sold the house and I finally moved the bed, an orange had fermented into the carpet and created a permanent stain.

The second and the most important reason for not eating in the bedroom is that the kids don't get to eat with the family and that's not good for building relationships.

3. Nothing happens in the bedroom that is against the family values

This may mean that a romantic partner isn't allowed in the bedroom at all, or at least not with the door shut – this is your call as a parent.

Likewise, if they are gaming too much and not going to bed until the early hours of the morning, then they shouldn't have their computer in their room. Sounds like 'whoa – don't be ridiculous, I'm not 13 years old'. No, they're not, but I'm sure you want to raise children who don't become addicted to anything or do anything that could damage their lives.

As parents we need to help them not be in a position where temptation ruins a good intention or a good reputation.

LESSON 73:

Encouraging business skills in children

Children and teenagers can be encouraged in entrepreneurship from a very young age as long as we don't molly-coddle them. A few common examples of early entrepreneurship are paper rounds, flipping hamburgers, mowing neighbourhood lawns, washing windows, babysitting, housework and coaching younger students.

They learn to put a value on their time

When my daughter Catherine was about 15, she wanted to save money for a school trip. She was already doing babysitting for a neighbour and a few occasional gardening and housework jobs. She decided to look for extra work after school with a local hairdresser. After a couple of calls – I was very proud of her; she was nervous about making the calls but did it – she managed to secure an after-school job sweeping the floor and doing very basic tidy-up work at a local salon. The first week passed and then came pay day.

She looked at the pittance in her hand.

'I could make more than this in two hours working for Mrs Shalfoon,' she said with disgust. The next day she handed in her notice.

Opportunities abound everywhere for our children if they're given encouragement. Here are two more examples, both farming ones.

Case study 1

James was 14. His dad owned 400 hectares (about 1000 acres) of very hilly sheep and beef land. It was before quad bikes became fashionable; horses were the primary transport around the hills. James seemed to have been born with a natural eye for business opportunities. One day he said to his father: *'It's silly to keep buying horses, Dad. All we need is a stallion and we can breed our own replacements. I've seen a stallion advertised – can you take me to have a look?'*

His father could have listed the normal problems associated with stallions. For my non-farming readers, these include broken fences (stallions are notorious for busting through fences when an alluring on-heat mare is in a nearby paddock), they're usually more temperamental, and it's another hungry mouth eating pasture that could feed several cows and a lot more sheep. However, Father supported the kid's initiative.

Yes, the horse was suitable. Now, how to get him home?

A few days later, once the horse was shod, James rode his new stallion home across country by himself. It was a journey of at least six hours, most of it off-road. How easy it would have been to pay for a stock truck to ship the stallion home; a young lad riding a strange horse home by himself, along rough tracks and through bush, would worry many parents. Yes, there was a risk, but his father knew he'd raised a responsible lad who was good with horses. Plus, everything comes with a risk... people get killed in cars every day.

Within two or three years James was breaking in his own colts and selling them to fund his studies at university and subsequent overseas travel.

He had a number of other teenage entrepreneurial schemes:

- Breeding sheep dog puppies and selling them to the local farmers.
- Hopping over the fence of his country school at lunchtime to buy stock at the sale yards next door, and after school helping his dad drove the animals the six kilometres to the farm.

At 24 he bought the farm from his father and some years later upgraded to a better-producing farm.

Today this man is driven by a 'best practice improvement' focus. He's constantly dreaming up new money-making and process-improvement ideas in a bigger arena than just his own farm. By age 31, he was elected by the farmers in his region to be one of six directors to Beef + Lamb New Zealand, a major national agricultural industry board. By 37 he was its youngest chairman. I'm proud to say that he's my son.

Case study 2

It's not just full-time farming families who see the benefits to their children of mucking in with the good, the bad and the ugly of farm chores.

A young woman I met on a trans-Tasman flight a few years ago was the daughter of one of New Zealand's senior captains of industry. As well as owning one of New Zealand's most profitable companies, the family also owns a very large farm not far out of Auckland. In her growing-up years, the family spent many of their weekends on the farm.

When she was about nine she asked her parents for a dog. 'Sure,' was the reply, *'as soon as you can kill its food.'* In less than a year she was competent at slaughtering a sheep and had her dog.

You might find that story a bit alarming or confronting. No doubt I'm showing my pragmatic country upbringing here, but personally I have huge admiration for her parents. She easily could have been a spoilt princess – but her parents gave her the gift of responsibility.

So it's no surprise that before the age of 30 she was managing director of one of the family's offshore companies, had a large staff, and was fully involved in all the family enterprises.

LESSONS 74:

Rules for graduating students

Some time ago a delightful list of life rules for graduating students passed across my desk, attributed to Bill Gates. Here's a shortened version of what our boy Bill is supposed to have said. (See who really wrote it at the end.)

Rule 1: *Life is not fair – get used to it!*

Rule 2: *The world won't care about your self-esteem. The world will expect you to accomplish something BEFORE you feel good about yourself.*

Rule 3: *You will NOT make $60,000 a year right out of high school. You won't be a vice-president with a car phone until you earn both.* [These days nearly every young person has a mobile phone and some do start on really good money, but the list was created back when $60,000 was a lot of money and mobile phones were far less common.]

Rule 4: *If you think your teacher is tough, wait 'til you get a boss.*

Rule 5: *Flipping burgers is not beneath your dignity. Your grandparents had a different word for burger flipping; they called it opportunity.*

Rule 6: *If you mess up, it's not your parents' fault so don't whine about your mistakes. Learn from them.*

Rule 7: *Before you were born, your parents weren't as boring as they are now. They got that way from paying your bills, cleaning your clothes and listening to you talk about how cool you thought you were.*

So before you save the rain forest from the parasites of your parents' generation, try delousing the closet in your own room.

Rule 8: *Your school may have done away with winners and losers, but life HAS NOT. In some schools they have abolished failing grades and they'll give you as MANY TIMES as you want to get the right answer. This doesn't bear the slightest resemblance to ANYTHING in real life.*

Rule 9: *Life is not divided into semesters. You don't get summers off and very few employers are interested in helping you FIND YOURSELF. Do that on your own time.*

Rule 10: *Television is NOT real life. In real life people actually have to leave the coffee shop and go to jobs.*

Rule 11: *Be nice to nerds. Chances are you'll end up working for one.*

I liked what I read. It fitted with my own child-raising philosophy, as you've already read. I was all ready to expand on Mr Gates' delightful bit of home-spun wisdom in a newsletter to my Top Time Tips ezine readers. But as I was about to share the list, I thought I'd better check the source. It takes nothing away from the value of the rules above, but I've added a rule of my own.

Robyn's Rule: *Don't believe everything you read in print. You could be dreadfully embarrassed.*

If you take a look at www.snopes.com/language/document/liferule.asp you'll find a very interesting overview of how the authorship of this list has morphed. Bill Gates has never claimed it as his; presumably someone other than the original author foolishly thought it added extra credibility. The true author is Charles J Sykes, who wrote the 1996 book *'Dumbing down our kids: why American children feel good about themselves but can't read, write or add.'*

In this day of instant information at our fingertips it's way too easy to take something off the internet and, because it's reproduced by a reputable source, assume it's correct. Even the most experienced journalists and editors can get it wrong.

And since we're talking about children, let's teach them also not to take everything they read or hear at face value.

LESSON 75:

Time management for teens

When Yvonne started MIOMO, her programme to help teens become independent, I ran the time-management part of her programme. She has now changed the format and integrated all the elements that used to be delivered by a range of presenters, including me. So if you think that some of the tips are things I talk about, you'd be right. We think alike on many things and regularly trade tips and ideas.

She's identified 10 big time-challenges for young ones. Here's her list and I've included her expansions of two of them. You'll get the full explanations and strategies in *Parenting Yadults*.

The biggest time challenges for yadults are that they:

1. *Find it hard to grasp the big picture, to set goals and to 'work with the end in mind'.*
2. *Don't plan and prioritise their activities.*
3. *Get caught up with instant rewards and lack discipline for long-term gratification.*
4. *Do what's urgent instead of what's important.*
5. *Underestimate how long it takes to do things or get somewhere.*
6. *Procrastinate and leave things to the last minute.*
7. *Can't find things when they need them.*
8. *Over-promise and over-commit – they find it hard to say no.*
9. *Are easily distracted from the vision or the task at hand. Don't finish things.*

10. *Don't schedule time off to play and refresh, or take a reward for a goal completed.*

Challenge 5: They underestimate how long it takes to do things or get somewhere.

Do you have a yadult who's always running late? Does she beat herself up constantly for letting people down? Does he blame the traffic, someone else or the weather, for being late for work or for arriving late to Grandma's birthday party? Sometimes this annoying habit is a form of passive aggression (giving the person a type of control over the situation and other people), but mostly it's simply that your yadult doesn't know his or her capacity for getting things done.

Try doing a 'time and motion study' with your yadult. For example, how long does it take your daughter to get ready in the morning from the moment she gets out of bed to walking out the door? She probably has no idea, so get her to time herself. How long does she take to have breakfast, have a shower and wash her hair, dry and style her hair, put on her make-up, get dressed, gather up her things and leave the house? I did this exercise myself and was surprised that the whole process took me about 10 to 15 minutes longer than I thought – and that's without stopping to check my email, Facebook or text messages.

A similar exercise can be done for travel to work or university. How long does it actually take? Consider the changing weather conditions, days of the week and any other factors, such as buses running late or traffic holdups.

Teach your yadults the principle of creating margins in their lives. A margin is a buffer or 'fudge factor' that gives you breathing space. You can use margins with time, money, and even in building relationships. Allow extra time and then work backwards from the deadline. For example, if your son has to get an assignment completed by the 31st of the month, encourage him to set his own deadline for the 30th, or even the 29th, to allow a buffer zone. If he doesn't need it in the end, he can take the day off and sleep in until noon.

Challenge 8: They over-promise and over-commit. They find it

hard to say no.

This challenge is about energy management. Often it affects people (as kind-hearted as they may be) who tend to be 'people-pleasers'. In some cases, they are people who simply have no understanding of their personal limits and regularly stretch themselves beyond their capacity. A good time to talk to your yadult about this is when she or he is worn out from over-doing it and desperate for a solution.

Teach your young one these clever phrases

1. *'I would love to help, but I need to check my diary first. I'll get back to you in the next couple of days.'*
2. *'As much as I would love to do that for you, I am a bit stretched at the moment. Sorry. Come back to me in a month (or a year).'* (Or just leave off the bit about coming back at all.)
3. *'Thanks for asking me, but I won't be able to do that with what's on my plate at the moment.'*
4. *'I am flattered that you asked me, but I don't think I am the best one for the job.'*

These responses are probably not in the language that your yadult would use – but you get the idea. It's important to have some lines rehearsed so that she or he doesn't get caught unprepared.

LESSON 76:

Parents are not the bank

Advice from Yvonne Godfrey

Many parents feel obligated to go guarantor because no one else will take the risk. And that's exactly what you need to consider – the risk. You may have a responsible young adult who already has a good track record with money. But remember, with all loans there is always the possibility of not being paid back. Likewise with going guarantor; if they don't pay, you will have to. If you are loaning money or going guarantor, loan the least amount possible. If it is for a car, the vehicle only needs to get them safely from A to B – it doesn't need to be a 'chick magnet' or a dragster!

Loaning money to your yadult

Parents are often seen as a nice source of interest-free finance. The problem is that not only is the money generally interest-free, but it also rarely gets recorded and, more often than not, it doesn't get paid back. $10 here, $50 there – it all adds up. Depending on your financial situation, these amounts may not break your bank, but that's not the real problem. The real issue is, when is the teenager going to learn that what we borrow needs to be paid back? When are they going to learn to live on a budget and learn the value of delayed gratification?

   A great starting point is to assess how much money they owe and write it down. Then negotiate the amount you want them to repay and when. You may decide to be generous and not ask for the full amount; that's your prerogative. However, I strongly encourage you not to wipe the debt entirely. It doesn't help them to become independent if you waive their debt and let them continue in their old pattern of spending *money on things they don't really need.*

If it's credit card debt, for example, you may wipe some of the debt, but then insist that they cut up their credit card or not buy anything on hire purchase. Agree on realistic repayments and set up an automatic payment plan.

See also:

Lesson 13: *If they damage something, they pay*

Lesson 69: *Preparing our teens to manage money in the big wide world*

LESSON 77:

Will your children be rich or poor?

I really like this great article from another friend, Stuart Fleming. It's practical commonsense, yet not very commonly applied.

A friend of mine has one son at primary school. Recently his class had a careers day, with several parents visiting to share how they earn a living. At dinner that night, the boy took great delight in telling his mother what he had learnt about the role of a doctor, a fireman, a lawyer, an accountant, a sales rep and a computer technician.

His mum smiled and agreed that there were lots of jobs to choose from, but inside she was puzzled; not one of the adults who spoke to the class were self-employed. When she mentioned that detail to his teacher the next morning, the response was one of pure surprise.

'Goodness, you're right!' exclaimed the teacher. 'I never even thought about self-employment as an option!'

Are your children exposed to financially imaginative options, or are they only exposed to the traditional thinking of 'go to school, get a job, save some pay, buy stuff, retire'?

Half of all students who enrol at university don't finish their degree. The concept of 'a job for life' is historic. Today's student is very likely to work in a role not even created yet!

So what does all this mean for their bank balance? It means that financial literacy from a young age is just as important as the skills of reading, writing, using technology and solving problems.

Given we live in a world where change envelops us – think credit crunch, rise of terrorism and climate shifts – I meet plenty of parents (and teachers!) who readily admit their money management skills aren't able to cope with the external pressures they face.

Petrol goes up in price. Ouch! Food products are more expensive. Ouch! Mortgage rates rise. Ouch!

One of the scariest questions I can ask a parent is 'Do you want your children to have the same level of financial confidence and ability as you?' Their eyes widen in horror as the realisation hits them; they are the fiscal role-model for their kids.

This is often a vicious cycle, because we may have not learnt sound wealth-creation strategies from our own parents. Being rich is somehow taboo.

Having skills in creating, spending, saving, donating and investing money are vital for the overall self-confidence of children. Rather than being dependent on their parents, or their employers, or the government, financially savvy young adults have greater choice and are more resilient to the uncertainties of a changing world.

Five ways to develop money-mastery in your children

1. *Never, ever, ever, ever, EVER laugh at any money-making idea your child comes up with. Ask them questions instead.*

2. *Play What-If? A simple game of questions: 'What if you weren't able to go to university – what would you do?' or 'What if people paid you for your top skills – which talent would you choose to hone?' or 'What if you didn't need more money – how would you spend your time?'... And let them turn the questions back at you too!*

3. *Hunt out and share stories of financially successful people you admire. What do they have in common? What habits do wealthy people never have?*

4. *Develop a system to teach the value of a dollar. I use the Four-Part Money Mastery system, which divides income (whether it's pocket money, birthday cash from Grandma or wages) into Spending, Saving, Donating and Wealth.*

5. *Give your children opportunities to take on financial*

responsibility. If the class is planning a field trip, can they manage collecting the bus money? Is your teenager capable of budgeting their entire weekly spending? (They'll have to do it when they leave home, so now's the time to teach them how!)

I bet your kids have plenty of off-the-wall, never-seen-the-light-of-day-because-they're-so-wacky, risky-but-fun ideas for making a dollar or two. Encourage them to develop their financial imagination!

[Reprinted with permission from Stuart Fleming]

SECTION VIII:

BONUS TIME MANAGEMENT TIPS FOR EVERYONE, NOT JUST PARENTS AND CAREGIVERS

In this section I've included a number of topics that don't strictly fit with child-raising but have an impact on home life as well as business. I trust you'll find them helpful.

LESSON 78:

How good are you at multi-tasking?

I can remember the days when, as a woman, I used to smile complacently when multi-tasking was mentioned. There'd be little quips such as, *'We know guys can't think of more than one thing at a time. Ask them something really important when they're watching TV and you'll never get an intelligent answer.'*

Guys, you have the last laugh. There is now a heap of research to show that constant multi-tasking is not so smart – and I've participated in some of it.

Researchers such as New York-based Basex have given us some startling data. For some years they were a research company devoted to helping us navigate the minefield of knowledge management in our over-informed world. Their chief analyst, Jonathan Spira, told me that an average knowledge worker loses about 28% of their day or 2.1 hours a day to constant interruptions.

It's not just the interruptions, which might only be very brief, that cause these startling figures.

Another problem is the switching time. Add up all the seconds in a day spent changing mental gears as we move from task to task and we discover serious productivity loss.

The amount of lost time is related to the length of the interruption. Basex identified that it takes between 10 to 20 times the length of the interruption to get refocused on the previous task. In other words, a 30-second interruption can easily take us off-task for five to 10 minutes. But it gets worse.

The next problem is the number of times we don't get back to the previous task. As we all know, once our train of thought is broken there's a very good chance that we don't return to a prior activity.

Don't believe me? How many open emails and applications do you regularly have on your computer during the day? Or how many items of paper or equipment are on your desk, waiting for you to decide where to put them? What actions or activities are awaiting a final decision or completion?

And what happens when we live constantly in a world where everything is going at warp speed, with multiple distractions? Think of many modern offices. There's constant low-level (or sometimes high-level) noise and movement. Phones ring, people walk by, emails ping as they arrive, and conversations happen all around you.

My friend and associate Steuart Snooks in Melbourne, who specialises in helping people conquer email overload, had this to say:

'A common result is pseudo ADD, a term coined by two Harvard psychology professors to explain addiction to the bombardment of information. They've noticed that many people experience shortened attention span because of the forms of communications used today. This has a sustained negative neurological effect as well. It isn't an illness; it's purely a response to the hyper-kinetic environment in which we live.

'So when a manager is desperately trying to deal with more than he can possibly handle, the brain and body get locked into a circle where the brain's frontal lobes lose their sophistication. We get black-and-white thinking and we start to lose perspective and shades of grey. People with this sort of difficulty struggle to stay organised, to set priorities and to manage their time. They experience a constant low-level feeling of panic and guilt.'

Paul Chin is another commentator on this issue of information overload. He says:

'Rampant multi-tasking and the deluge of available information has [...] created a paradox. The more we try to do, the less we get done. And

the more inundated we are with information the less time we spend absorbing it.'

Perhaps women can cope a little better than men when it comes to complex multi-tasking But – it's not smart to even try. Both genders get frazzled, exhausted and frustrated when they've got too many things going on at the same time. And they lose hours in a day.

So, congratulations to the people who stay focused on one thing at a time! Keep it up. You'll get your work done faster than your multi-tasking colleagues.

If we bring the discussion back to managing our family life, you'll have already come across various tips in this book on being focused on one thing at a time.

If you'd like more ongoing practical observations and suggestions, register to receive notification of my reasonably regular blog at www.gettingagrip.com by grabbing your copy of my free ebook *How to Master Time in Only 90 Seconds*.

Also, I've got a very special audio download, only for readers of my books, at http://gettingagrip.com/digitalgifts.

Have you downloaded them yet? (I mentioned them at the beginning of the book.) You'll find five hours of interviews with five of the world's top thought leaders on efficiency and productivity.

- You'll be amazed at how easy it is to make time for exercise (with Lauren Parsons, fitness and wellbeing expert, whom I've already introduced you to in the food section of this book).
- How to control your inbox with information-overload expert Steuart Snooks
- An interesting perspective on goals and great advice

on simplicity (and much more) from world-renowned blogger Leo Babauta.
- How to manage major projects by award-winning Dr James Brown, ex NASA project manager.
- And from Olympic multi-gold medal coach Mark Sutherland and me, as we share tips on how to overcome the *'too much to do and not enough time'* syndrome.'

LESSON 79:

Is it possible for parents to enjoy any level of work/life balance?

Work/life balance is given a lot of lip service in the corporate world. What does that really mean? How is it played out in the business world? And is it just a pipe-dream for parents of young children?

Typically there are three distinct stages of a person's working life.

1. The single person's or young married phase of hard-out, long hours, where the imperative is to build a career. These folk are striving to carve their niche and are prepared to be virtually married to the job.

2. The mid years when a person typically has family responsibilities and a mortgage. They're beginning to realise that in order to have a life outside of work they have to take responsibility for it; it's a very rare employer who will mandate that their staff have sufficient time away from work. The employee (or business owner in many cases) might not yet have worked out the balance issue, but they're becoming more aware of the importance of it and looking for ways to build it into their lives.

3. And then there are the mature years, when a person tends to be confident in their particular expertise. They may shift from one company to another, but with grey hair comes the commonsense philosophy: *'I'll give work my all when I'm here, and my other interests and family will dictate the hours I'll do and the level of commitment I'll give the firm.'* They've shifted the priority order from 'work

first' to 'self and family first'. It's not selfish. Actually, the person who's married to the job is selfish – firstly towards their loved ones and secondly to the firm, for they're creating a dependency that can't be sustained long-term.

Is it necessary to wait until you're in the wrinkly brigade before you start to get a life? I don't believe so. Is establishing a work/life balance the responsibility of the company? Or is it up to us?

I was greatly impressed some years ago to come across Daniel Petre's book *Father Time: Making Time for Your Children*. (Since then he has also written *What Matters: Success and Work-Life Balance*.)

In earlier years he has been Managing Director of Microsoft Australia, then a VP at Microsoft HQ in Seattle, and later was sent back to Sydney to run the Asia-Pacific division of Microsoft, finishing there in 1996. Since then, he's started a number of technology companies and is also an investor and philanthropist.

In his early career Petre was a classic workaholic, but once children started to come along he began to take a deeper look at what fathering really is about. It dawned on him that modern corporations are, with a few exceptions, dysfunctional in what they expect from their staff, and especially their senior managers. As a result, he dramatically changed his way of working – and yet was still able to hold down senior executive positions.

He became very concerned about the way so many men have abdicated their fathering roles, some consciously but many because they don't see any other way. And so he began to observe and study the whole issue of what work/life balance really means, initially in the context of fathers who miss out on much of their children's developmental years. These days, with so many working mothers, his concerns apply to both genders.

Following are a few quotes from Daniel Petre's book *Father Time*

- *Long hours are wrong hours.*
- *A rested worker is a better worker.*

- *Long hours invoke the law of diminishing returns and a shorter life.*
- *We reward people for the wrong things when we applaud and reward them for long hours. Instead, reward them for doing the job quickly and efficiently, and for leaving work at a sensible hour.*
- *The job is never done – accept it.*
- *Work obsession. Men (and women) have, over the last 50 years, created business infrastructures that are anti-children, anti-family, anti-spouse, anti-community, and anti-social responsibility. They work so long they have nothing left to give.*
- *To use profit as the only measure of success is a very narrow perspective.*

I really recommend the book if you've ever wondered whether there is a less crazy way to 'do' life and also create a good living. Petre not only shares a great many thought-provoking facts but also comes up with some solutions, a number of which I've arrived at independently and you'll find sprinkled through this book.

It is possible to work hard, hold down a good job AND have a life – but you have to plan for it. Life balance does not happen by accident.

See also

Lesson 2: *Count your 'hats'*

Getting out of the office

LESSON 80:

Do we need to work such long hours?

Some years ago I ran a series of 35 seminars all around New Zealand for small-business owners, on behalf of one of the major banks. One of the recurring themes was how to work fewer hours. Some people were doing it, some were looking for ways to do it, others thought they were locked in and had no choice but to work crazy hours – sometimes seven days a week.

The conversation in one regional centre was particularly vigorous. Dave owned an automotive care business

'I used to open Saturday mornings as well as the usual five days. One Saturday afternoon, as I rolled home exhausted yet again, it hit me like a bomb that every weekend I was too tired to do anything with my family. All I wanted was rest; it seemed the weekend had just begun when Monday showed up.

'I got to thinking – if I felt like that, my staff probably did too. Was that fair to them? Then I asked myself what would happen if we didn't open on Saturdays? Would it damage the business?

'I decided to take a bold step, risk losing business, and stop Saturday trading. That was five years ago. It has made no impact at all on the company profits and my staff and I are much happier.

'Customers just organise themselves better. They make sure their automotive needs are handled during the week. I don't stay open late either. The shop shuts at 5pm, and the customers fit in with me.'

That started a very spirited debate. We had several people in the room with seven-day businesses.

'I've got a maintenance business, servicing the needs of large 24/7 manufacturing plants. I have to be on call all the time. We're only a small firm and that's the way it is.'

'We've got a restaurant. We finally took a weekend off, the first one in six months, and left town. That morning the chef arrived over an hour late and another staff member called in sick.'

Hands started shooting up all over the room. We'd touched a raw nerve.

Here are a few comments from others who'd reached similar conclusions to Dave.

Tony had a distribution business. *'The owner of probably my most successful outlet is always away having holidays and long weekends,'* he told us. *'He's trained his staff well, they're empowered to make decisions, and he can leave them to it.'*

Paul had trained his small team of five to cover each other's work – their business was inspecting cars for mechanical safety. His daughter ran his office; she also could do the car inspections. At any time, one person could be away and the business would keep running smoothly.

Another lady shared how she and her husband had run many businesses, including a number of seven-day-a-week operations such as hospitality and a convenience store. With the store, they were initially open from 5.30am – 8pm. Within a short time they were feeling half-dead, leaving no energy for their small children.

Eventually a business advisor asked if they really needed to keep such long hours. He suggested tracking the number of customers they had each hour to see if there was anything they could change.

For a short time they rang off the till every hour, just to get a clear picture of the trading. (This is a basic business principle – you can't improve what you don't inspect.)

'Very quickly we decided to chop an hour off each end of the day. We found smarter ways to do things; for instance, my husband stacked the pie warmer the night before. We quickly realised that the people who used to be our impatient first customers at 5.30am were the same people who waited at the door at 6.30am. The people who always came in late, *just as we closed at 8pm were the same people who came late at 7pm.'*

The woman sitting next to her believed it was important to have the confidence to take control of their businesses and working conditions, including opening hours. *'If we don't set out clear expectations,'* she said, *'we've only got ourselves to blame.'*

What do you think?

My take? I'm with Dave and co. I know for sure that if we keep working crazy hours, something will give. Machines don't work well for long without maintenance; nor do we.

The solutions aren't necessarily obvious to see, but they will be there waiting to be discovered.

LESSON 81:

How to stretch time

I know it sounds weird, but we can 'stretch' time.

The following techniques can be applied in both home life and business.

Schedule the important people into your week

Ask people what they value the most and they'll usually say family and health. But when you ask where they spend most of their time and focus, it will be work. Often the justification is: I'm working to support my family.

Of course that's important, but how many people do you know who say things like: *'I'll spend time with the kids when I can find some time'*, *'I'll take a holiday when things get quieter at work'*, or *'I'll get back to exercise when this busy time is over'*?

This is a guaranteed recipe for problems. There will never be 'spare' time to fit such priorities in. We need to block in the priorities first; the work will fit around them.

If you don't block in 'special' time with your special people, they'll eventually get tired of waiting.

Do you know the old song by Harry Chapin, *Cat's in the Cradle?* The little boy, waiting for his ever-busy dad to spend time with him, kept saying, *'One day I'll be just like you'*. When his dad was an old man, longing to see the son who never came, he found that indeed, the promise had been delivered.

If something is important enough to be treated as an appointment, and scheduled into your organiser, it will almost always happen. It may be that you have to reorder some work activities in order to fit in personal and family priorities.

However, in almost all cases the work will fit around the priorities of someone who's clear on what really matters, and acts accordingly. If you wait for 'spare time' you'll never have it.

For simple tips on how to do this, see:

Lesson 27: *Make a list of family priorities to help sort the lengthy 'to do' list*

Live in the 'now'

Today many have forgotten how to live in the moment. Most of us make bedfellows of stress and anxiety. We focus either on the past – pondering on what has already happened and what we could have done better – or on the future – planning or worrying over coming events. We're so busy squeezing more activities into every moment that many of us forget to be 'present' with what we're currently engaged in. We therefore lose the joy of the experience. And so time seems to race by in a frenetic and out-of-control way, because we're not 'in' it.

I had a great example of this from a school secretary on one of my training courses. Every morning she'd arrive at work, keen to get to the tasks of the day. Then, as you'd expect in a busy school office, people of all sizes started coming at her. By about 9.30am, when the rush died down, she'd find herself feeling frayed, frazzled and frustrated because she hadn't yet started on the 'to do' list.

This went on for some months, until one day she realised that she, not the situation, was the source of the frustration. She became aware that in order to enjoy her work she needed to change her attitude; the requirements of the job were not going to change.

Her solution? She accepted that 'busy' was the way it was, grabbed a cup of coffee first thing in the morning, mentally girded her loins for the onslaught and settled in at the front desk, ready to go with the flow. To her delight, she found that those first two hours became one of the best parts of the day. Everyone had a good time, and once the traffic died down she could get onto her 'to do' list, happy and feeling effective.

For two experiences of my own, see also:

Lesson 33: *What I learnt about stress management from a pack of kids*

Lesson 40: *What my grandsons taught me about multi-tasking*

Change your language

Notice your words and how the people around you speak. How often do you hear *'I'm so busy'*; *'I can't fit it in'*; *'I have no time'*; *'I'm always late/overworked/tired/have too much to do'*? Speak it and you'll get it!

Instead of hearing *'I'm sorry I'm late again'* slip off your tongue, try words like, *'I apologise for being delayed. I had to complete something'* or *'I was held up at the last appointment.'* It might sound like we're playing with words here, but a reframe of your language helps to reframe your sense of control and well-being, as well as your future expectations of yourself.

As much as you can, use affirmations or future-focused positive statements of intention like *'I'm getting much better at my time management'* or *'There is always enough time to do the things that matter.'* This seemingly simple technique was one of the methods that transformed me from 'chronically late' to 'world specialist on time management'.

See also:

Lesson 85: *'Oh, they're always late!' – How we process time*

An attitude of gratitude

Practise honouring the moment. Develop a sense of gratitude for the gift of life, for the gift of small things. A useful exercise to reinforce this habit is to write a journal entry every evening on *'Five things I was grateful for today.'*

Enjoy the mundane – it stretches time

Next time you wash the dishes or the car, mow the lawns, feed the children, sort out the paperwork on your desk, or any other simple task, enjoy the activity for itself. Try not to spend the time your body is occupied in thinking about something else. Don't wish the task was completed – honour the moment and the experience. You'll finish more relaxed.

Time will stretch/expand instead of leaving you with the feeling of hurry, pressure and impatience often felt with a mundane task. And many times you'll be surprised to find that it was a pleasant duty instead of the chore you didn't really want to do.

Meditate

Learn to meditate, or if this seems too hard, try every day to sit quietly for at least 10 minutes and focus on a plant or some other object. As thoughts drift into your mind acknowledge them and let them go. Breathe deeply from your abdomen, mentally saying *'breathe out'* with every outgoing breath and *'breathe in'* with every incoming breath.

This helps you to slow down to the natural rhythms around you and create peace and time 'space'.

LESSON 82:

How to still have energy at the end of the day

How often do you go into an energy slump in the early afternoon and find yourself thinking how much you'd love to have a quick nap? Do you follow your body's cues – or do you follow society's expectations and stick at your desk?

If the latter is your normal experience, perhaps some of the following experiences might sound familiar as you endeavour to push through that tired space:

- Your patience with your children disappears.
- You can't think straight and every little annoyance seems like a mountain of frustration, causing you to snap and snarl.
- You're working at a keyboard and suddenly your efforts are punctuated with a ridiculous number of typos.
- Your normal level of energy has just flown out the window. You're feeling exhausted, sometimes quite suddenly.
- You might be yawning.
- You're working at about quarter speed.
- Concentration is a challenge; you find yourself re-reading information you would normally scan and comprehend swiftly.
- You notice you're thirsty, hungry or uncomfortable in some other physical way.

In my role as an international time-management specialist, I work with people from all around the world in just about every sector and at many levels of seniority, including CEOs, senior executives and owner/operators of small to medium businesses.

Because sanity gaps are part of my message, I almost always ask my audiences if they take a regular lunch break, and how many take tea breaks – not just the 'grab a cuppa and take it back to the desk' kind of tea break, but a real one where they give their brain a rest – away from their desk. (Think of it as 'defragging' the brain instead of the computer.)

Typically, more than 70% of the room, many of them knowledge workers, tell me they don't do either on a regular basis.

The next questions are *'How effective are you in the afternoon?'* and *'How tired are you at the end of the day?'* The look on people's faces is classic – often a bemused *'Why didn't I notice that connection before?'*

Why we slump in the afternoon

A range of biological rhythms flow through our body, running on differing cycles. One is ultradian rhythms. Loosely translated, ultra = many and dian = day – the many rhythms of the day. They cycle continuously through our body like rolling waves. Typically the up side is about 45 minutes, down for 45, and then a flat spot at the bottom of 15 to 20 minutes before starting on the next up cycle.

The flat spot at the bottom of the cycle is *not* a negative thing – instead it's the rest cycle that our body needs in order to recharge, rebuild and to grow. If we keep pushing through these bottom cycles, if we don't give our body a chance to recharge, we push the poor old thing into flight or fight mode. The consequence? You already know: stress, burnout and eventually sickness. Without exception, every person I've challenged on this has agreed that when they push through those down cycles of tiredness, thinking perhaps that they're being lazy or that it's not appropriate to slow down for a short while, they become less effective in the afternoon and end up dragging their weary bodies home at the end of the day – not much use to themselves or the loving family waiting for their quota of time.

It's also a fatigue-management and safety issue. We see

messages about fatigue on our roads – the same message should also be shouted in the workplace. Many of the worst accidents we've seen in modern times have occurred at the end of long shifts – Chernobyl is just one example. And that applies to knowledge workers as well as physical workers.

The problem is, it's not only young parents whose children wake them up through the night that are sleep-deprived; it's become the norm for much of society. Almost all of us are awake for longer hours than a century ago, because of electricity.

Add to that the impact of an increasingly global economy and the advent of the internet and modern telecommunications. Since the 1980s many people have an increasing sleep deficit.

Do you know – or are you – someone who:

- Never turns off the phone?
- Keeps the mobile phone beside the bed and accesses it for work-related matters through the night?
- Takes a laptop home almost every night in order to get more work done?
- Works across borders and has to get up early or stay up late to talk to colleagues or clients on the other side of the world?

So what to do about it?

Morning and afternoon tea breaks and a lunch break away from your desk – that's the first and most simple solution.

Also I actively encourage everyone to nap when they're tired - on the job or at home. For many of us, it will only be once a day, or not even every day, but if it needs to be more often, just do it. It really is only for a few minutes each time, and the payback is huge. Many very efficient Western business people regularly take a short nap in the early afternoon.

I'm using the word 'nap' but you could equally call it a meditation. A maximum of 20 minutes is all we need to recharge.

In that time our brain slows down to the alpha state, very similar to meditation. Any longer and we'll probably drop into a deeper sleep, which won't give the same kind of benefit. Coming to after 15 to 20 minutes we might feel a little dozy for a couple of minutes but then we're up and away again, operating at top efficiency for the rest of the day. And having taken a break, many of us are also more creative.

Power napping is what kept Winston Churchill operating at full steam through all those tough World War II years. He was meticulous about his daily power nap of about 20 minutes. He would stretch out in a special nap chair or pop upstairs when he was working at Downing Street. In the Houses of Parliament he had a bed.

Other famous names who applied the same habit meticulously include Margaret Thatcher, John F. Kennedy, Beethoven, Benjamin Franklin, Leonardo Da Vinci, Salvador Dali, Eleanor Roosevelt, Brahms, John D. Rockefeller, Robert Louis Stevenson and Albert Einstein.

There's another benefit. Have you noticed that the best ideas never come when you're sitting at your desk? How often is a brilliant idea or the solution to a problem sitting in your mind when you wake up in the morning? Imagine tapping into that resource through the day. Often it is when we nap that fresh ideas, new insights and solutions rise to the surface of our mind. According to the Salk Institute for Biological Studies, naps enable our brain activity to remain high throughout the day. If we fail to take a nap, our brain activity declines.

Einstein knew this. He was very deliberate in his use of power naps to help solve problems. He would relax in a comfortable chair or on a sofa, his head propped on one hand while holding a handful of ball bearings in the other. When the hand relaxed enough to drop the ball bearings into a conveniently placed bucket he would wake up and quickly write down whatever was in his mind. Many of his most brilliant ideas came to him in this alpha state or twilight zone. He relied on the noise of the falling ball bearings to bring him back to full consciousness; to have slept longer would have taken him into deep sleep.

Here's the thing – the desire for a nap in the early afternoon is normal. But countless people, especially Westerners from cooler climates, have been socialised since the Industrial Age to ignore the messages their bodies try to give them.

It's time for those of us in industrialised and North European-style business communities (including those in the Southern Hemisphere, such as Australia and New Zealand) to rethink this habit. I believe we need to take a lesson from the smart folk in the warmer Mediterranean countries (with their restorative afternoon siestas) and also the Chinese. Did you know that it's normal practice in China for people to nap at their workplaces, including corporate offices, after lunch?

'But I work in a corporate environment and can't take a nap', you might be saying. Try asking, or think laterally.

Maybe it's a lunch-time nap under a tree in summer, as I did as a teenage librarian recovering from glandular fever. Can you lie down in the sick bay during your lunch break? That was my trick when expecting my first baby and still working. Or, what about driving your car to a nearby park or shady tree and pushing the seat back for 10 to 15 minutes?

These days my napping is not related to mothering or recovery from illness, but in order to have high energy for my audiences. I often arrive early to a client engagement, park nearby, put my phone on silent but set the timer (it will then only ring for the timer, not any calls) and have a short zizz. I don't care if attendees or clients see me – the messages from my body are more important than what someone else might think. And anyway, I'm practising what I preach.

In the 1990s, NASA started experimenting with short naps for their astronauts during their workdays. Performance skyrocketed. Nowadays the 'NASA' nap, or a variation, is a common practice for many international pilots.

More and more companies are catching on to this zero-cost productivity boost. Nike, Google, NASA, Ben and Jerry's, Zappos and Huffington Post are just six of an increasing number of corporations who provide quiet rooms that their employees can use for napping, meditation or just to take a short break – but no talking.

And of course, if you work from home or are a full-time parent or caregiver, you are the boss. You've just got to organise yourself and your children instead of a resistant employer.

As I wrote this section I was looking after three of my smaller grandchildren for a few days while the parents had time out. The youngest is only two. I was exhausted after a busy morning at the museum but they had all the energy in the world. So I took a nap while the girls played in the back yard with the gate securely shut. It's amazing how you can train your consciousness to jump to full alert if the sounds change, or things have gone too quiet! Twenty minutes of light repose with a couple of checks inserted into that time and I was back to high energy to cope with the evening bustle.

See also:

Lesson 30: *How about a little lie-down?*

LESSON 83:

Too tired to think straight? Be a better procrastinator!

(*In earlier parts of this book I've touched on some of the concepts outlined in this lesson, specifically related to child-raising. Here, I've approached the concept of taking time out from an adult perspective.*)

You thought procrastination was a naughty word, didn't you? You're only partly right.

Negative procrastination – putting off until tomorrow that which should be done today – is an energy-sapper. It occurs when we allow trivia to block us from having a fulfilled, happy and productive life.

On the other hand, *creative* procrastination is good. I love explaining it – it's like telling people that sometimes chocolate and ice-cream are actually good for you! It is deliberate – pushing back on low-level tasks in order to stay focused on higher-value activities.

> *Creative procrastination is putting off until tomorrow that which won't advance your life plan by being done today. It's the planned and deliberate gift of prime time to yourself regularly, doing what gives you greatest satisfaction, including doing nothing if that's your choice. It's also learning how to leave undone those things that didn't really need to be done, so that you achieve balance and satisfaction in your life.*
>
> From my first book *Getting a Grip on Time*.

We have been brought up to regard *'doing nothing'* as bad. Is it? How about adopting a new paradigm about *'think'* and *'play'* time?

Back in 2005 I read an interview by Sean O'Hagan of the Observer conducted with British psychoanalyst and writer Adam Phillips, author of *Going Sane*. Phillips had a refreshingly different perspective.

Here are some excerpts from the interview

Phillips: *One of the best things we could do as individuals is allow ourselves to daydream more.*

O'Hagan: *In this belief, of course, [Phillips] is in direct conflict with the thrust of our culture, which is geared to ever more activity; longer hours, more multi-tasking, always the need to keep up, or run at full pelt to try and catch up.*

Phillips: *One of the more distracting things about capitalist culture is that there is no stupor, no time to vegetate. What I would suggest is more time-wasting, less stimulation. We need time to lie fallow like we did in childhood, so we can recuperate.*

O'Hagan: *It seems to be dawning on us that, although our lives are easier – that is to say, less poor, less threatened by disease and death, less prescribed by class, gender or race than the lives of our parents or our grandparents – they are nevertheless more* **pointlessly complex** *and, as a result, we seem to be more unhappy. That unhappiness manifests itself... in a strange dissatisfaction with ourselves, and in our inability to be, for want of a better word, contented.*

(You'll find the full interview at www.guardian.co.uk/books/2005/feb/13/booksonhealth.lifeandhealth)

These guys made sense to me. You've probably also noticed the same paradox – that material wealth for many equals time-poverty and constant discontent. Just because we can fit more in doesn't mean we should.

Here's a question for reflection: How can we make life simpler and enjoy it more?

A few thought-starters

1. Before taking on another commitment, ask yourself: *'Does this fit with the life I choose to live?'*

2. Are you saying 'no' to enough things?

3. When you're about to buy yet another 'thing', stop and ask, *'Is this item going to make my life richer, or will it just make life more crowded and complicated? Is it a 'need' or a 'want'? Will it quickly become clutter?'*

4. When did you last review your goals? No time like the present if you haven't! (More on this in the next lesson.)

5. Is there anything else you can do to simplify your life? For example, what can you give away, recycle, discard?

6. Are you blocking free weekends into the diary now – no commitments – every four to six weeks?

Three more actions that might be helpful

7. Turn off the TV. Don't let it dominate your evenings. What messages are you putting in your sub-conscious just before sleep?

8. Give your mind time to slow down before you sleep. (While I love reading, I rarely read business books at night – they wire me up too much. Instead, before bed is novel-reading time – a delicious daily treat.)

9. It may seem like a contradiction, but plan to do nothing. Make sure you've left *'fallow'* time in your week, every week, and hopefully every day.

Less is more.

See also:

Lesson 32: *Every six weeks have a 'do nothing' weekend*

LESSON 84:

Family goal-setting

How often have you started a new year with the intention to write down your goals for the coming year, but somehow you never get around to it? If that sounds at all familiar, you'd be in good company with over 90% of the population.

So why is it that so few actually get around to recording their goals in some form? Could it be that the good intentions weren't translated into more specific goals? And were they written down?

You might like to think about these issues

About 30% of people say things like:

- *I don't have time.*
- *I don't know how.*
- *I've got a pretty good idea of what I want but it's just in my head.*
- *My work goals are set by the boss. I'm not sure what I want in my personal life.*
- *I might fail to reach it.*
- *What if I succeed? Can I cope with the changes that will bring?*

And – more than 60% will say: '*I don't really know what I want to set goals on.*' Their conversation often includes comments like:

- *Taking time to write down goals seems like too big a project.*
- *It feels as though it will take too long.*
- *I want to be sure I'm recording what I really want and I've been too busy to give it a lot of thought.*

If this applies to adults, how much more does it apply to young people? When parents and teachers aren't confident or knowledgeable about how to set goals, how are youngsters to learn?

At the time of writing this book, I've specialised in time management for 24 years. Never at any time has my opinion changed about the MOST IMPORTANT factor in the topic: a clear set of comprehensive written (or pictured) goals. If we don't have that starting point, how on earth can we make the best time choices when other options (often masquerading as new bright ideas or other people's requests) present themselves?

The most powerful time management tool we have is the ability to say '*no*', not in a career-limiting or relationship-limiting way, I hasten to add. (Read my free report *How to Master Time in Only 90 Seconds* at www.gettingagrip.com if you'd like to know more about that.)

However, if we either don't know what's really important to us, or we're not putting any focused energy into things we give lip-service to, how do we know what to say '*no*' to? Instead, we'll find that time has quietly slipped away, leaving us with a vague feeling of dissatisfaction. We'll find ourselves majoring in minor things and those half-formulated dreams will be pushed back – yet again.

Setting – and achieving – your big picture goals

1. Find a quiet spot.
2. Don't attempt goal setting with other people making noise around you. You must have 'alone' thinking time.
3. Think as far into your future as you can – at least a year out and ideally much further ahead.
4. If something comes into your mind, don't dismiss it as impossible or impractical. Instead, listen to your intuition.
5. Initially, set goals for yourself, not the significant others

in your life. It's not selfish – it's just easier. If other people will be involved with some of them, negotiate later. Some things may have to be shifted out a bit but you need to be clear on your own thoughts before you can have a useful conversation with your loved ones.

6. Nothing is too small or too large. A small thing can sometimes be the trigger that leads to the fulfilment of a much bigger goal.

7. Don't limit yourself – forget 'realistic' for now. Dream big. It isn't your imminent tasks or relatively easy projects we're interested in at this stage. They come later. 'Realistic' is entirely too limiting for long-term dream goals. Who wants to be realistic? Or only choose goals that are easily achievable? How boring!

8. Write your goals down. Many people will say, *'Oh, I know what's important to me. Why do I need to record it?'* Have you noticed that the exercise of putting your thoughts down on paper forces clarity?

9. Be very specific. Don't say *'I want more money'*, *'I want a new house'*, or *'I want to travel'*. Set an amount of money you want. Describe what the house will look like. How many bedrooms does it have? Do you want a garden? Where will you travel? For how long? What specific activities do you wish to do when you're there?

10. Find or make pictures to represent your words and thoughts. Make a collage, a poster, a vision board, a scrapbook or some kind of visual reminder. Pictures are incredibly powerful. Put them wherever you'll see them constantly – it might be your fridge, your office wall or maybe your bathroom. After a while they'll become wallpaper and you'll hardly notice them most of the time. However, the message continues to impact your sub-conscious. It might take some years, but you'll be amazed at the result.

A family suggestion

Get the whole family involved. You might each do your own personal one, and then another group one for the family. Kids love creating collages and once you get them into a goal-setting habit, you'll have given them a life-long gift.

LESSON 85:

'Oh, they're always late!' – how we process time

Have you ever been driven to distraction by other people's time habits? Do some members of your family have a different approach to time than you?

Your frustration is probably because they process time in a different way. From my observation I believe we're born with a bias to one way or the other, although it can be modified with focused effort, if necessary.

The behavioural science Neuro-Linguistic Programming (NLP) uses the terms 'in-time' and 'through-time' to explain this.

An in-time person is great at being present **in the moment**, very focused on what's under their nose, but struggles to manage their long-range time focus. Their ability to mentally detach and forward plan is minimal. They often find it very difficult to predict how long an action will take and therefore they're often late for deadlines, activities or events. Their strength is in being fully focused on what's in hand. Their weakness is that they're often late for things and this can cause disruptions.

On the other hand, through-time people are **more objective about time.** They're able to detach, to see themselves outside of the events they're involved in. They seem to be effortlessly punctual, able to plan ahead, to estimate how long they'll need for any activity. Their strength is their ability to plan and anticipate. Their weakness is that, because of their ability to detach, they're sometimes perceived as aloof and uncaring. Also, they sometimes struggle to fully enjoy the present moment because they're always thinking about future events.

Because opposites attract, intuitively seeking the qualities they lack, couples are frequently a mix of styles. As you can imagine, this often causes huge frustration – until they learn to understand and compensate for each other! The least in-time member of the partnership almost always takes responsibility for the family's time-keeping. They're not trying to irritate each other with their time habits, but often do.

Through-timers, I'm sorry, you can't single-handedly change your in-time mates. They have to do it for themselves. It might be useful to show them this lesson though. You, on the other hand, may need to learn more about relaxing, going with the flow when it doesn't *really* matter what time you get somewhere. Practise being more focused on the 'now'.

In-timers, here are five strategies to help you overcome the negative consequences of your style.

The good news is – we can modify behaviour to make life easier for ourselves. And if we have in-time children, we will need to help and coach them as they learn to apply the techniques for themselves.

1. Whenever you catch yourself saying, *'I'll just do this one thing more'* – DON'T. Intuitively you know it will make you late, but you've become used to blocking that thought.

2. Start with the end in mind. Consider what time you want to be somewhere and then count back the minutes, including drive time, parking time, can't-find-the-keys time, a toilet break, coffee and last-minute interruption time. Then add on an extra 15 minutes as a safety net. You'll be shocked at how much earlier you have to leave! I really encourage you – just try it a few times. You'll be delighted with the stress-free feeling you experience at the other end. What you're doing at a cellular level is creating an earlier trigger to tell you it's time to get going.

3. You're probably reading this and thinking, *'But I'll waste time by getting there too early!'* It's unlikely, but just in case, take something to read or work on while you wait.

4. When you've had a punctuality 'win', notice your feelings of success and calmness. Hear the congratulations of surprised friends or workmates. See yourself arriving relaxed at your destination. Anchor those feelings and thoughts. The next time you're tempted to last-minute, remember how success felt and act accordingly.

5. Don't worry about total change in one hit – it seems too big! Just concentrate on one task at a time, one day at a time. Make a mission of being on time for one thing each day. One day you'll look back in amazement and realise that you're now regularly on time for almost everything.

You might be wondering how I can describe so accurately the feelings and experiences of an in-time person. Very easy – I used to be one! For years I struggled and was constantly late, but the good news is … I won!

Every now and then I break out, especially if it's a social occasion and it doesn't really matter what time I get there, but these days it's quite rare for me to be late.

If you teach your in-time children these techniques you will make their lives much easier.

A LAST-MINUTE PS!

LESSON 86:

The best and fastest way to give your children a great start – and dramatically reduce the risk of allergies and other subsequent health crises

My book designer had nearly finished the layout of this book when I realised I'd forgotten a really important tip.

In an ideal world, this final lesson should be in the first section of the book, but completely re-organising the layout as we neared the end of production is neither possible nor practical. (Take this as an example of pragmatic time-efficiency, and my apologies if it slightly annoys your tidy mind!)

I'd just spoken at a conference where nearly a third of the 200-plus bodies in the room were under the age of two. The little ones were quiet and very well-behaved; if an occasional baby was momentarily unhappy the mother quickly took it out of the room.

The relaxed baby/toddler-friendly atmosphere took me right back to the years when I always had a baby or toddler on my hip and often a bump out the front, and spent regular time in a similar environment. La Leche League, the organisation running the conference, had been hugely influential in the way I raised my children. Given how much I'd learnt from the members all those years ago, I was shocked at my memory-lapse, but the association had been off my radar for a long time. It was only because I'd been asked to contribute my professional time management expertise that my grey matter had a jiggle-up.

So what is this really important tip?

Do everything you can to breastfeed your baby. Nature does know best.

When I was pregnant with Chris, my first baby, I was lucky enough to be invited to a La Leche League meeting. It's a world-wide organisation that supports mothers who wish to breastfeed. Being helped by qualified coaches and learning from other mothers going through the same issues was and is the fastest and most relaxed way to acquire mothering skills. For young mothers who grow up in modern Western societies, very few of us have the chance to learn from more experienced mothers; our friends are typically our role models.

Chris would probably have been on the bottle within six weeks if I hadn't attended that first meeting and hadn't had friendly support only a phone call away; I was desperate and confused, with a crying baby who wouldn't settle. Instead, my new friends taught me how to breastfeed him until he self-weaned on to adult food.

Breastfeeding saves so much time and work, is quick and easy once the baby is established, totally hygienic, safe, portable, always at the right temperature, on tap if the little one is hurt or hungry, and it's the easiest way to bond. And those are just a few of the advantages.

If you feed your babies the way nature intended, which is until they're weaned, if you introduce solids as their digestive system develops along with their teeth, you never spend a penny on formula, very little or nothing on mushy tins of processed baby food, and they'll have far less chance of developing serious health complications at various stages of their life, including allergies.

Reducing the risk of allergies

How many people do you know with allergies? Have you ever

wondered why there seems to be so much more of it around these days? In earlier years it was rare, yet today it's so common that whole industries have grown up to support the sufferers. If any family you're closely linked with has allergy issues, how much time, money and energy is consumed every week, and what is the day-to-day impact on both the sufferer and the family?

At the conference mentioned above, I had the opportunity to listen to allergy researcher and author Maureen Minchin https://infantfeedingmatters.com. She had just released the results of decades of research from working with families of allergic children. She is convinced that a lot of the problems link back to what we feed our babies, right from birth. According to her research, long-term allergies can be triggered by even just a few bottles of formula when the baby is new-born. (There is much more to it than this one point, of course.)

Maureen Minchin's research is available in her book *Milk Matters*. Actually, it is really three books. Book 1 shares research showing that immune damage is being acquired vertically, compounding inter-generationally, through early infant nutrition; and that infant nutrition is the single most important contributor to the diseases of 'modern' societies.

Book 2 documents the ongoing real life experiment of infant formulas, and their known and emerging consequences for lifelong health. It reveals frightening facts from industry-funded research and explodes the pervasive myth that industrial products are 'nearly as good' as breastmilk.

Book 3 links the science and history to everyday infant problems like colic, reflux, disturbed sleep and allergies of every kind, giving practical advice about current controversies and how to prevent or resolve such diet-related distress in young children. Parents will get most of what they need from just this third book, but researchers will want to check her sources. You'll find them expanded and discussed in the first two books.

Those who read any part of the book or listen to her presentations will be convinced of the necessity of enabling women to breastfeed their children, and the urgent need to provide women's milk for children whose mothers cannot do so. See the bibliography for more information about Minchin's work, as well as other resources and information.

Where is the support to be found? And why is bottle-feeding so common?

Bottle-feeding has its place - as a backstop - but almost every woman can breastfeed until the baby weans, *if* she gets the *right* information and support. This includes those who choose to go back to work, although that is easier if the workplace is breastfeeding-friendly.

Thank goodness, many hospitals, midwives and support systems have come a long way since I had my babies, but ... sadly, many women are discouraged from fully breastfeeding their babies until they wean naturally onto big-person food. This is largely due to wrong information and inaccurate and misleading advertising from powerful, wealthy and very well-resourced commercial interests. They state or infer, that infant formula is as good as, or nearly as good as, breastmilk. However, dig into the huge body of research around the subject and a different story emerges.

If we follow the money trail the reason why is obvious; formula producers are only in business to increase profit to their balance sheets. From their perspective, of course they'd take the easy option, with vulnerable and easily influenced parents as a soft target. The long-term health of our families and communities is way down their list of considerations. Very poor social responsibility, I suggest. Tobacco companies have the same ethics. (Please note: I'm very much for dairy farmers and dairy companies making profit. However, I question the morality of excessive marketing of processed milk powder as a baby food. There are other things we can do with milk powder.)

For parents to make informed choices, it is vital that they have access to accurate information and support about how to breastfeed when situations are more complex, such as multiple births, sick babies, ill mothers or physical complications. They also need to know the latest research about the adverse impact of formula feeding. Apart from the risk of allergies, a few of the other impacted health issues include increased tendencies to obesity, diabetes, childhood asthma and other pervasive modern diseases. On the other hand, there are a myriad of benefits to mother and baby from breastfeeding, including reduction of cancer risks for the mothers.

And I'm not even going to start on the morality (or lack of it) that aggressively pushes third world mothers to formula-feed their babies. See the World Health Organisation's paper listed in the bibliography for enough information to curdle any milk in range! For example, *'only 44 per cent of the world's newborns are put to the breast within one hour of birth. Even fewer infants under six months of age are exclusively breastfed.'* Read more and you'll see how many babies die needlessly as a result.

For help with all breastfeeding matters, I strongly encourage you to reach out to your nearest La Leche League group or similar. In Australia, for instance, the Australian Breastfeeding Association is a sister organisation. Worldwide there are an increasing number of resources and people to help fight this particular health battle against commercial self-interest. See the bibliography for contacts.

LOVE IS EVERYTHING

At the beginning of this book I promised to tell you about the second pivotal experience relating to time, as I raised my young children.

In the early 1980s I lived in a small country community. There was great turmoil in my life. I had six beautiful children, but everything else was tipping on its axis. I didn't know what to do, which direction to go.

In this state of tumult I was invited to attend a 21st birthday party in my local community. As I sat watching the dancers swirling and swinging I noticed Mr and Mrs Davenport. With two grown-up sons they'd been surprised with a late addition to the family, a young lad who was the age of one of my younger sons, five years old. Laughing, happy, they whirled joyously around the floor, enjoying and loving each other.

A few weeks later, Mrs Davenport was dead – from a brain tumour.

The little community was shocked and devastated. For me, although I was distressed for the family, it also delivered another message. It drove home to me that we really do only have one chance at this life and no one knows the day it will be taken away. Life is a precious gift; we have a duty, as well as the opportunity, to live it to the full.

Soon after, I made a decision that changed my circumstances dramatically. I stepped into the unknown – fearful, frightened and unsure, but knowing at a very profound level that I was doing the right thing.

Life has delivered some surprises and lessons along the way but I have never ever regretted my decision, no matter how tough things sometimes were.

There will be times as a parent when you wonder if you're doing the right thing. It may be to do with your child-raising techniques. It may be to do with schooling decisions. It may be about where you live. Should you take a transfer? Could you move to another country? You may be in difficulties with your marriage. There may be serious health challenges for one or more members of the family. The infinite diversity of our human experience delivers every challenge we could think of and then some! The ideal of a happy and prosperous life, a great marriage and happy and healthy children is lovely – but that's not everyone's reality.

Trust your heart, follow your intuition, pray for wisdom and guidance, love your children, and know that a happy and fulfilled parent makes for a happy child. They're resilient little souls and even though they also suffer through our sufferings, your honesty with them, as well as a genuine search for the right path for yourself, will bear fruit.

It's not about the money. It's not about trying to live the perfect life. Instead it's about the love, the experiences, the openness and the honesty you share with them. It's about making the most of every day, enjoying this gift of time, this gift of life. We pass this way but once – be in it.

I wish you joy with all the wonderful young people in your world. They are a gift and our future.

ACKNOWLEDGEMENTS, BIBLIOGRAPHY AND USEFUL RESOURCES

Section I: Start as you mean to go on - reflections on effective parenting

Lesson 3: Pills are not the answer

Richard DeGrandpre. *Ritalin nation.* WW Norton, 1999.

Robert Whitaker. *Anatomy of an epidemic.* Broadway Paperbacks, 2010.

David Fox. *Change your life.* Balboa Press, 2010.

Tony B. Rich and Meg Jordan, PhD, RN. *Mother's Little Helper: The history of amphetamine and anti-depressant use in America.* www.wellcorps.com/Mothers-Little-Helper-The-History-of-Amphetamine-and-Anti-Depressant-Use-in-America.html.

'From 1935 when Benzadrine Sulfate first appeared to entice doctors to prescribe amphetamines to housebound women tired of their daily drudgery, through chemical manipulation and rebranding, into the fastest-selling drugs to children and young adults, the history, evolution and morphology of amphetamine usage in America is eye-opening. Find out how this category of chemicals, designed for weight loss and improved mood in the '60s, and then banned for sale to adults due to its health hazards and addictive qualities, is now the leading prescription medication for ADD and ADHD in children and the drug of choice for high school and college students across America.'

Website: www.madinamerica.com

'Mad in America's mission is to serve as a catalyst for remaking psychiatric care in the United States (and abroad). We believe that the current drug-based paradigm of care has failed our society, and that scientific research, as well as the lived experience of those who have been diagnosed with a psychiatric disorder, calls for profound change.'

Lesson 4: Extend those children – movement is vital

Sophie Foster, Jumping Beans http://jumpingbeans.net/

Jamie Morton. *Obesity study asks if under-5s active enough.* New Zealand Herald, July 10th 2016. www.nzherald.co.nz/lifestyle/news/article.cfm?c_id=6&objectid=11669947

'In April 2016 the New Zealand Ministry of Health published an expert group's review, which made a series of strong recommendations including that toddlers and preschoolers should get at least three hours of physical activity each day and should be sedentary for no more than one hour at a time. The group further recommended that children under two should have no screen time, while for older children screen time should be limited to less than an hour a day.

'Auckland University obesity expert Professor Boyd Swinburn said a comprehensive approach was needed to reverse New Zealand's fast-growing childhood obesity rates. Children were getting fatter around the world, but our own kids were growing obese at "an [alarming] rate".

'One third of school-aged Kiwi children are overweight or obese. High rates of obesity in under-5s have been identified. NZ children's health is now in the bottom third of all countries.'

Lesson 6: Don't mollycoddle them – kids need to learn resilience and self-control

Richie Poulton, *Childhood Self-Control: a key component of resilience?* http://www.ecc.org.nz/Folder?Action=View%20File&Folder_id=349&File=KEYNOTE4Richie_Poulten.pdf

Leonard Sax M.D., Ph.D. *Boys Adrift: the five factors driving the growing epidemic of unmotivated boys and underachieving young men.* Perseus Book, 2007, updated 2016.

Dr Scott Duncan, AUT Human Potential Centre (State of Play Survey) https://www.persil.co.nz/wp-content/uploads/sites/10/2015/11/AUT_State_Of_Play-141015.pdf

Lesson 9: Parenting for independence

Karen Boyes. Blog article: *Parenting for maturity and independence.* 2016 www.spectrumeducation.com/parenting This website includes many excellent resources for parents and teachers, plus her blog is really good.

Lessons 15 & 16:

Maggie Mamen. *The Pampered Child Syndrome – how to recognize it, how to manage it, and how to avoid it. A guide for parents and professionals.* Jessica Kingsley Publishers, London. 2005, rev. ed. 2006.

Lesson 17: The consequences of child-centred upbringing

Children with more self-control turn into healthier and wealthier adults. http://dunedinstudy.otago.ac.nz/news-and-events/article/6

Why Am I? What determines our personality, health, wealth and happiness? https://www.tvnz.co.nz/ondemand/why-am-i/episode-1-6474579 Also, Richie Poulton's research cited in Lesson 6 above.

Lesson 19: What we can learn from the French about raising children

Pamela Druckerman. *Bringing Up Bébé – one American mother discovers the wisdom of French parenting.* Penguin, 2012.

Section IV: Tips and techniques for daily efficiencies

Lesson 36: Teach everyone to become a 'walking question mark'

Frank B Gilbreth Jr and Ernestine Gilbreth Carey. *Cheaper by the dozen.* T.Y. Crowell, 1948; HarperCollins, 1963, 1993. Perennial Classics, 2002.

Robyn Pearce. *Getting a grip on the paper war.* Reed Publishing, 2003. Available from www.gettingagrip.com

Section V: Fast and healthy food - yes, you can have both at the same time!

Lessons 58, 60, 63:

Lauren Parsons. *Real Food Less Fuss: the ultimate time-saving guide to simplify your life and feel amazing every day.* 2016. www.RealFoodLessFuss.com

From a highly credentialed well-being specialist, this is THE layman's guide to eating well yet with ease and speed. It's perfect for families coping with budgets, time constraints and kids. It is also the most practical and easy-to-read treatment I've ever found on the topic of nutrition.

Lauren demystifies all kinds of wrong beliefs about healthy eating, gives really simple guidelines and practical tips that work. She also includes a good range of easy time-saving and low-cost recipes.

On a different but related point, if you're strapped for time and feeling guilty about not getting to the gym or more regular exercise, look at her 12-week online programme www.gettingagrip.com/lauren I love her concept of snacking on exercise. Basically, she explodes the myth of needing to work out an hour at a time in order to make progress. A few minutes a day of the right combination of exercises can make an enormous difference. And - every one of them can be done in your own home without any special gear.

Section VI: A few observations on technology over-use

Lesson 67: How is screen time impacting your children?

Aric Sigman. *Remotely Controlled: How television is damaging our*

lives. Vermilion, 2007.

Aric Sigman. *Time for a view on screen time.* Archives of Disease in Childhood. British Medical Journals. Nov 2012 Vol 97 Issue 11:935 – 942. Full article at www.researchgate.net/publication/232222451Time_for_a_view_on_screen_time.

Aric Sigman. *Visual voodoo: the biological impact of watching TV.* Article published in Biologist. Feb 2007 Vol 54: 1. Full reprint at www.aricsigman.com/IMAGES/VisualVoodoo.LowRes.pdf

Section VII: Raising teenagers without pulling your hair out

Lessons 70, 72, 75, 76:

Yvonne Godfrey. *Parenting Yadults.* 2015. http://www.parentingyadults.com/

I have enormous respect and admiration for Yvonne Godfrey. She runs MIOMO – Making It On My Own. http://miomo.com/, a very powerful 4-day life skills and leadership programme to help teens transition smoothly into adulthood. And as you will have read in this book, I strongly recommend you get hold of her really practical and informative *Parenting Yadults*.

Lesson 77: Will your children be rich or poor?

Stuart Fleming is a professional speaker and workshop leader specialising in team training and change management. He's an enthusiastic believer in independent teens, with many years of involvement in the Scouting movement. www.linkedin.com/in/stuartfleming

Section VIII: Time management tips for everyone, not just parents and caregivers

Lesson 79: Is it possible for parents to enjoy any level of

work/life balance?

Daniel Petre. *Father Time: making time for your children.* Macmillan, 1998.

Daniel Petre. *What matters: success and work-life balance.* Jane Curry Publishing, 2004.

Lesson 81: How to stretch time

Stephen Rechtschaffen. *Time shifting.* Doubleday, 1996.

Lesson 82: How to still have energy at the end of the day

Arianna Huffington. *Thrive.* WH Allen, 2014.

Lesley Gillett. *Sleep your way to success: working smarter in the information age.* Time Out Seminar Company, Australia, 2001.

Jim Loehr & Tony Schwartz. *The power of full engagement: managing energy, not time, is the key to performance, health and happiness.* Allen & Unwin, 2003.

Lesson 83: Too tired to think straight? Be a better procrastinator!

Robyn Pearce. *Getting a grip on time.* Reed Publishing, 1996. Multiple reprints. Gettingagrip Publishing, 2012. Now available at www.gettingagrip.com

Sean O'Hagan. *That way sanity lies.* Interview with Adam Phillips, author of Going Sane. www.guardian.co.uk/books/2005/feb/13/booksonhealth.lifeandhealth)

Lesson 85: Oh, they're always late!' – how we process time

Tad James & Wyatt Woodsmall. *Time line therapy.* Meta Publications, 1988.

Lesson 86: The best and fastest way to give your children a great start – and dramatically reduce the risk of allergies

The following resources just scratch the surface.

La Leche League New Zealand www.lalecheleague.org.nz

La Leche League International www.llli.org/

Australian Breastfeeding Association www.breastfeeding.asn.au/

Pinky McKay, Australian lactation consultant, author and blogger. www.pinkymckay.com/about-pinky/ If you're feeling conflicted about breast versus bottle, do read her article at www.pinkymckay.com/not-breastfeeding-not-guilty-2/

Breastfeeding-friendly workplaces and how to return to work with a breastfed baby. http://canbreastfeed.co.nz/workplace/ www.breastfeeding.asn.au/bf-info/breastfeeding-and-work/

Maureen Minchin. To learn more about Maureen Minchin's work, written in easy-to-understand language and also supported by a vast bibliography of sources, check out her website https://infantfeedingmatters.com and a presentation she made at www.ilactation.com/present. Her message is of vital importance to all parents and health professionals.

Also, in a number of countries, many hospitals now have very experienced and certified lactation specialists attached. Many others work directly in their communities. More about this at www.ilca.org/global-health/partners and in New Zealand www.nzlca.org.nz

Further information can also be found in many World Health Organisation publications. www.who.int/nutrition/publications/infantfeeding/breastfeeding_advocacy_initiative/en/ is one. Less than 40% of children worldwide under six months of age are exclusively breastfed, with devastating results for children in many third world countries.

Other contributors

Kate Booker – a good mate from my Sydney days with huge experience as a nanny in a prior life.

Lisa Rose, mother of a blended family of six, including twins. familymattersnz.wordpress.com

Heather Douglas www.bizbuzz.co.nz/

Diane Lithgow – a regular contributor to my blog

Margaret Lyall

Other writers have written to me directly or contributed to my blog over the years. Unfortunately I don't know everyone's full names to acknowledge here, but I give you grateful thanks.

General parenting sources:

The Parenting Place www.theparentingplace.com/

Ian and Mary Grant, founders of The Parenting Place www.fatherswhodarewin.com/

Steve Biddulph. *Raising boys.* Finch, 1997. 4th ed. 2013.

Michael Grose www.parentingideas.com.au/Home

Diane Levy. *Of Course I Love You ...now go to your room!* Random House, 2002.

Rachel Martin, mother of seven and blogger - http://findingjoy.net/

Allison Mooney. *Pressing the Right Buttons.* Random House, 2007 (2008). Allison's engaging perspective on how to understand different personalities is relevant to both adults and children.

Getting a Grip on Time Management

By Robyn Pearce

Do you run frantically in ever-decreasing circles? Does your family complain that they never see you? Do you ever wish for time management help from someone who really understands the problems? Then this easy-to-read and commonsense approach to time management by a reformed time-waster is for you!

You will discover many practical real-life ways to:

- Distinguish between urgent and important
- Get a handle on when to do what
- Move from reactive to proactive
- Overcome time-wasters
- Delegate well – gain time by involving others more effectively
- Overcome procrastination

'I was told this book is really 3 books in one. I would almost say it is nearly all the books I've read about time management, goal setting and effective habits in one. Easy to read and full of practical ideas.' **Elle Anderson**, Business and Life Coach.

Purchase now at www.RobynPearce.com/books

About Time: 120 tips for those with no time

By Robyn Pearce

Have you ever thought: 'There must be a quicker way?'

Are you challenged by too many time choices, too much to do, but don't have enough hours in the day?

This book is a 'quick-dip' of tried and true practical tips from real people – tips that will help you find those missing hours.

Included are tips on how to:

- Overcome procrastination
- Work more effectively with others
- Manage your computer efficiently
- Get back your life, even if you work from home
- Turn meetings from time-wasters to time-savers
- Handle paper and information more efficiently

'*I keep* **About Time** *in my car and dip in whenever I'm waiting for my kids. Pure gold.*' **Susannah Bernstein**, lawyer and mother.

Purchase now at www.RobynPearce.com/books

Getting a Grip on the Paper War: managing information in the modern office

By Robyn Pearce

How often do you stop at your desk, look at the teetering piles of paper, and either threaten arson or feel like hiding? The 'paper war' is fought by millions of people every day – and you can win it!

Robyn Pearce's no-nonsense advice will give you:

- Fast easy ways to handle paper & electronic information
- Increased productivity and much less stress
- The most efficient filing systems for you
- Less clutter screaming 'Deal with me now!'
- Fast reading and reduced reading piles
- An efficient home office
- … and much more

'I feel like I've been given the keys to a large end V8 after sitting in a trumped up shopping trolley waiting for the lights to turn green...' **Phil Mitchell,** Insurance Officer.

'The light has gone on! It isn't rocket science, but until you read a logical step-by-step book like this, the obvious isn't obvious. My desk has never been so tidy and work so up to date, even at the end of the month.' **Gail Leighton,** Office Manager, Accounting Firm.

Purchase now at www.RobynPearce.com/books

Getting A Grip On Leadership
How to learn leadership without making all the mistakes yourself

by Robyn Pearce and LaVonn Steiner (USA)

Leadership specialist LaVonn Steiner (USA) and multi-title author Robyn Pearce (New Zealand) bring you lessons learned the hard way, starting from little or no leadership experience. No time is wasted on academic theories with limited real-world relevance. Instead they focus on real-life ideas and examples you can use immediately.

A practical guide to leadership - without all the jargon!

- Beat the fear of trying new things
- Build a positive work climate
- Help your team pull together to a common goal
- Enjoy the journey, with your team, to leadership mastery
- Think strategically
- Improve performance and productivity

'Required reading for everyone ... clear, practical, and easy to read ... gives readers guidance on actual implementation... Section on strategic planning with tracking tools the best I've seen.' **Linda Knodel**, Snr VP/Chief Nursing Officer, St. Alexius Medical Center, Bismarck ND.

' ..romped through your book in 8 days ... intend to refer to it many times in the future. The many concepts and ideas will certainly help me become a better manager.' **Steve Wangler**, Snr VP, Bank Center First

Purchase now at www.RobynPearce.com/books

About Time for Teaching:
120 tips for teachers and those who support them

By Robyn Pearce

Teachers and administrators in several countries share their 'best practice' ideas, interwoven with Robyn Pearce's delightful and relaxed time management wisdom.

- Stop the clutter of unwanted material
- Reduce interruptions
- Leave problems where they belong
- Have a life outside of school
- Enjoy your own kids, even after a hard day at school
- Hire the best staff
- Simplify and reduce meetings
- Get information back from others on time
- Educate over-enthusiastic board members
- Use technology to save time
- Find and use volunteers effectively
- Reduce panic and stress in unexpected situations
- … plus four chapters on efficiency tips for the school office

'Follow Robyn's advice. It makes a difference.' **Owen Hoskin**, Past Principal, Henderson High, New Zealand

Purchase now at www.RobynPearce.com/books

ABOUT THE AUTHOR

Robyn Pearce has learnt her skills and knowledge about time management and productivity from the ground up. In fact, she's made just about all the mistakes you could imagine, and survived!

From humble beginnings as a farmer's wife, mother of six (including an intellectually handicapped foster son), then a solo mother and real estate agent, Robyn had to learn better time management skills - or sink!

However, once she started to focus on improvement, she turned into a major strength. Since 1992, as a keynote speaker, trainer and author she has shared her experiences and knowledge with thousands of clients in many industries around the world, helping them win their time battles. As a speaker she holds the top accreditation of CSP (Certified Speaking Professional), held by less than 1% of professional speakers worldwide.

She's a prolific author, weekly columnist for the New Zealand Herald online, regular contributor to many journals, and a regular expert commentator on radio, television and online blogs and interviews.

At the GettingAGrip.com website you'll find all manner of further resources to assist you in your time-learning journey. Be sure to request your free report *'How to Master Time in Only 90 Seconds'* at her website www.gettingagrip.com

www.ingramcontent.com/pod-product-compliance
Lightning Source LLC
Chambersburg PA
CBHW050628300426
44112CB00012B/1711